P9-BIE-730

In Celebration of
Devil with A Briefcase

"What a refreshing perspective! Successful entrepreneurs today need to know when to color outside the lines. Supported by her own unique stories, Jan shares her take on when and how to do that."

–BRIAN E. WALSH PhD
Bestselling author of *Unleashing Your Brilliance*
www.UnleashingBrilliance.com

"Here's a book that is concise, easy to read and full of practical little known "secrets". Jan has managed to find balance between business and spirituality and makes it work!"

–KARE ZIGAY, www.prayerawakenings.com

"If most of us put even a portion of the energy, time and focus that the JWs do in spreading the word about their religion into our businesses, we would all be millionaires."

–DR. ANNE MARIE EVERS
Best Selling Author and Radio Talk Show Host
www.affirmations-doctor.com

"Devil with a Briefcase contains powerful strategies, tips and secrets to success like no other book has ever shared. You'll be fascinated by what you learn."

–MICHAEL LOSIER, Best Selling Author of *Law of Attraction*

"Jan Janzen's perspective is wickedly wry, straight on the mark, and a must read for anyone who operates their business from a place of heart and spirit. If you're an entrepreneur who wants to make money while actually being nice to people, read this book."

–LAURA HANDKE JONES, author of *Six Degrees to Your Dreams*
www.wishweavers.com

"Jan's book offers a most provocative and insightful look at doing business today. It's so refreshing to have such authentic perspectives to give my business a reality check."

– JOSETTE WILLIAMS, Health Coach

"Jan has written a masterpiece for entrepreneurs who strive to be the best at what they do! Using the controversial Jehovah Witnesses lessons and applying them to your own business, you will learn how to build a massive empire with eager and passionate employees and clients. If we could all develop businesses with these principles in mind, the success rate of small business start-ups would sky rocket!

–TROY WHITE, www.ProfitGrowthCoach.com

"Devil with a Briefcase is definitely no ordinary, snooze-fest type business book. Look out... because Jan Janzen doesn't pulls any punches when it comes to what it takes to succeed in business... but the stories are so much fun, you almost forget that she is giving you a good swift kick! "

–MICHAEL PORT
Author of the national bestseller, *Book Yourself Solid*

"I'll be referring Devil With A Briefcase to all my clients. The majority of small business owners I meet are struggling for success. Jan Janzen's wonderful book makes you think, laugh out loud, and teaches valuable success secrets. Male and female entrepreneurs will enjoy this book and the results they achieve by applying it's wisdom."

–LYNNE KLIPPEL, Author, Publisher, and Radio Show Host
www.lynneklippel.com

"Devil With a Briefcase is chock full of sassy, bright wisdom that will help you ramp up your sales, stamina, and strategy. Jan Janzen is no devil. She just might be your business' biggest angel."

–TAMA J. KIEVES, Best-Selling author of
*This Time I Dance! Creating the Work You Love
(How One Harvard Lawyer Left It All to Have It All!)*

"Jan has an amazing ability to engage the reader with personal stories and humor while opening their eyes to the realities of the entrepreneurial world. Read this book. It will awaken your entrepreneurial spirit and provide you with practical advice for reaching your potential as an entrepreneur."

–ANDREW BARBER-STARKEY, Master Certified Coach
Creator, ProCoach Success System
www.procoachsystem.com

"Who would have thought that one of the world's most scorned religions would have so many concrete lessons on running a successful business with focus and principle? It takes someone of the caliber of Jan Janzen to extract these lessons, without bitterness for what she experienced, and honoring the choices that she and each of us have made."

−SHEL HOROWITZ, award-winning author of
Principled Profit: Marketing That Puts People First
Founder of the Business Ethics Pledge
http://www.business-ethics-pledge.org

"I was VERY curious to learn about the Jehovah Witness way of life, and boy oh boy did this book deliver − not just on that, but on so many other things I hadn't anticipated! Even the idea of a content-rich business book written in bathroom reader format is brilliant, and although it's such a simple thing, it reveals the depth of understanding Jan has for entrepreneurs and the busy lives we lead. This is sheer business meat and potatoes, and definitely some food for thought I hadn't 'chewed' before. It's more than just a fascinating book... in true Jan Janzen style, it's an experience."

−KRISTA GREEN, Founder & CEO
Organized for Life Canada, www.organizedforlife.ca

"How many times have we winked and said "The devil made me do it", in an attempt to justify what we really wanted to say and do but just never had a reason to. Well, now you have a reason to with Jan Janzen's, The Devil with a Briefcase. By reading this book, you will gain the courage and the wisdom to make your own decisions, guided by one of the best "in the business". Her radical approach and "honest to God" advice will help you understand what it takes to succeed as a spiritual entrepreneur...in the here and now and the hereafter."

−RICHARD CASAVANT, Corporate Speaker and Facilitator
www.casavantconsulting.com

"For you to learn valuable information from a book that can help you with your business, it must be interesting enough so that you actually read it, understand it and then retain it. Jan's book is one of the few that does. This book truly captured and held my attention. I found it easy to read, funny, honest, authentic, and yet full of great advice and wisdom."

−BRENDA EASTWOOD, RNCP, www.BrendaEastwood.com

"As an entrepreneur who strives to model my business after my religious principles, I was a bit hesitant about reading this book due to the title. My curiosity won over and after reading Jan's book, I have to say that this is a must read for all entrepreneurs who struggle between balancing their spiritual values with the cut-throat world of business. Whether you're a Jehovah's Witness, Christian, Jewish, Muslim or atheist - if you're looking for a way to boost your business, get Jan's book right now."

–LEESA BARNES, Business Podcasting Expert, www.leesabarnes.com

"This is hard-hitting, cut-to-the-bone, real world information that will change your life for the better. Strap yourself in and get ready for reality. This is a best seller by the best seller I have ever met: Jan Janzen."

–ROBIN J. ELLIOTT, www.DollarMakers.com

"Devil with a Briefcase is the Spiritual Entrepreneur's bible for personal and business success. Jan Janzen shares her vast entrepreneurial and business successes with you. She combines her humour and experiences in an international, unorthodox religious movement with insider information on just how that organization also achieved enviable business growth and success. Apply the advice in Jan's book to prosper both spiritually and financially to succeed in today's business environment while maintaining your values and integrity."

–REV. IOHO DE BEER, Founder, Planet Peace Foundation,
Author of *Read and Grow Rich*

"You may not agree with certain aspects of any religion - but the analogies and insights Jan Janzen pulls together will certainly 'enlighten' your way of thinking about your business. Talk about the oooh-ahhh factor - this book has it."

–ELAINE ALLISON, International Speaker
Author of *The Velvet Hammer, PowHERful Leadership Lessons for Women Who Don't Golf*
www.thevelvethammer.com

"My gauge of a great book is how much of it I can implement into my business. Jan gets it and shares it so it makes sense...and I can profit. From the rookie to the veteran, every entrepreneur can use this book."

–WAYNE KELLY, www.onairpublicity.com

"This book gives you a MAP to a clear road to the top! You'll get inspiration & self-improvement tips that will spring board you to success! Jan's writing is captivating, straight to the point and straight to the heart. Her experiences as an entrepreneur are real, touching, witty and fun."

–CATHI GRAHAM, Best Selling Author,
Founder Fresh Start Metabolism Program
www.newfreshstart.com

"Working with Jan Janzen has dramatically altered both my business and my life in general. She has a way of getting you thinking about things in a completely new way. Her writing is informative and enlightening, while also being captivating and fun. Following many years and dollars spent on personal and business development, I now say that Jan Janzen is the individual who has made the biggest impact on my business life in a very long time."

–SANDRA LYNN LEE, Miracle Inspirations, LLC
www.MiracleInspirations.com

"Jan Janzen has written a book you won't want to put down! Devil with a Briefcase gives information and advice that every business person needs to know - whether you are just starting out or have owned a business for years. You'll appreciate Jan's straightforwardness and memorable stories."

–DR. EVELYN ZELLERER, Expert in Restorative Justice
www.ezellerer.com

"You can't help but get ignited by Jan's love and passion for life and wanting to bring the best out of everyone! Any entrepreneur would be nuts not to take this Devil's advice!"

–KIMBERLY EASTERBROOK, Intuitive Interior Stylist
www.tranquilplacesconsultinggroup.com

"Jan Janzen is an out-of-the-box thinker who has her feet solidly planted in business. Not only is she unveiling the business principles of an extremely successful religious organization, but is re-framing that information in a practical way that (as a spiritual entrepreneur) I can easily apply to my business. A most thought-provoking, enlightening and inspiring read!"

–GELI HAMILTON, Feng Shui and Energy Clearing Expert
www.consciousconnexion.com

"Whether you think you know how to run a business, or you are a brand new entrepreneur, this book has something for everyone. Unique stories combined with straight-to-the-point advice are yours for the taking."

—WANDA MARCH, Phone Skills Coach
www.callphonetalk.com

"Jan Janzen's book is like a lighthouse to those entrepreneurs who are floundering in a sea of confusion wanting to make a success of their business without the resorting to the attitude of 'winning at any cost.' This book shows entrepreneurs how to be tough and, at the same time considerate. And, I love the way the book is laid out. It didn't have to be read from cover to cover; I could simply focus on the chapters that were of importance to me now. Devil with a Briefcase is one book that I will be recommending at all our marketing seminars."

—ALFRED PETTERSEN, Co-Owner, Y2Agency Inc.

"Different, challenging, provocative and definitely controversial are some of the words to describe Jan's book. However, she is also right on the mark when it comes to understanding entrepreneurship. You'll think she's been spying in your office when you read this book."

—DARREN WEEKS, Founder and President
Fast Track to Cash Flow Inc.
www.fasttracktocashflow.com

"Jan's passion for life and for helping those around her achieve success (while sleeping comfortably at night) is so apparent in this masterpiece. Funny, witty, FANTASTIC and to-the-point are all ways to describe the treats awaiting you (and your business) inside! As an entrepreneur who aims to build a business stemming from fun, integrity and a desire to succeed, this book has become my prized tool for doing so. I can't wait to share Jan's wisdom in Devil with a Briefcase with all my clients."

—KRISTA GARREN, Superb Web Design
www.superbwebdesign.net

DEVIL WITH
A BRIEFCASE

101 Success Secrets
for the Spiritual Entrepreneur

Jan Janzen

Women Empowering Women Inc.
Vancouver, British Columbia, Canada

Limit of Liability/Disclaimer of Warranty: While the author has used her best efforts in preparing this book, the author makes no representations or warranties with respect to the accuracy or completeness of the contents of this book. The purpose of this book is to educate and entertain. It is designed to provide information about the subject matter covered. It is sold with the understanding that the publisher and author are not engaged in rendering legal, accounting or other professional services. If legal or other expert assistance is required, the services of a competent professional should be sought. The author and publisher shall have neither liability nor responsibility to any person or entity with respect to any loss or damage caused or alleged to be caused directly or indirectly by the information contained in this book.

Devil With A Briefcase
Copyright © 2007 Jan Janzen. All rights reserved.
No part of this publication may be reproduced or transmitted in any form or by any means electronic or mechanical, including photocopying, recording, or by any information storage and retrieval system, without written permission from the copyright owner.

Printed in Canada

Cover Design by Nu-Image Design
Illustrations by Animantz
Formatting by Proof Plus

Library and Archives Canada Cataloguing in Publication

Janzen, Jan, 1961-
    Devil with a briefcase : 101 success secrets for
    the spiritual entrepreneur / Jan Janzen.

ISBN 978-0-9735884-2-2

    1. Entrepreneurship. 2. Success in business.
        I. Women Empowering Women Inc. II. Title.
        HB615.J36 2007   658.4'21   C2007-900816-X

Publisher: Women Empowering Women Inc.

For information contact Women Empowering Women Inc. at
info@womenempoweringwomen.biz

10% of the gross total proceeds of this book will be donated to microfinancing organizations to support entrepreneurs in developing countries.

How to
Read this Book
Guilt-Free

I have purposefully kept the chapters short and to the point. Most of them can be read in 5 minutes or less. Please feel free to read any chapter in any order and know you will get a complete thought or idea. You can certainly start at Secret #1 and go through to #101 in order, but you can also open the book anywhere and just start reading.

Put the book on your bedside table and read a chapter or two every night, keep it in the bathroom and read a couple of chapters every day, or enjoy it while having a cup of coffee in the morning.

However, you choose to read it, I trust you will get the answers you need at the right time for you. Have fun with it, enjoy it and remember to laugh!

Jan

~ About the Author ~

 **Jan Janzen** has been an entrepreneur since the age of 19 when she purchased her first Molly Maid franchise. Today she is actively involved in the coaching, mentoring, and educating of entrepreneurs all around the world through her newsletter, teleclasses, CD's and consulting program.

Jan spent 38 years as an active Jehovah's Witness, including four years as a missionary in Ecuador, South America. In 1999, she walked away from the religion that she had known all her life. She lost everything, her friends, most of her family and her husband of 18 years, because of that decision.

However, as she started to analyze her entrepreneurial success, she realized that much of her success, if not ALL of her success, came down to the powerful principles, habits and systems that she had learned sitting for hours every week in a Kingdom Hall and spending thousands of hours knocking on people's doors.

Today as a veteran entrepreneur with over 25 years experience in network marketing, licensing, franchising, partnerships and corporations, and as a non-denominational minister with a very successful entrepreneurial business, Jan has written a one-of-a-kind guidebook for being an outrageously successful entrepreneur in today's complex world.

Devil with a Briefcase, 101 Success Secrets for the Spiritual Entrepreneur, along with her CD series for the Spiritual Entrepreneur that focuses on building profitable businesses based on ethics, values and fun, while making a difference in the world are the foundation of Jan's career.

www.janjanzen.com

Dedication

I dedicate this book to my parents who affectionately called me "The Mistake" for the first six years of my life. Looking back, I know it was no mistake that I was raised by parents who had just become Jehovah's Witnesses the year I was born.

I thank my mother for instilling in me her deep love of God and a profound appreciation for scripture. Although I haven't chosen the spiritual path she would have preferred, I am deeply grateful for the love and respect she showed for my decisions. I miss you Mom.

I thank you Dad for your example of drive, determination and success as an entrepreneur, and as a survivor of the religious persecution and poverty you experienced as a young child in Russia. I'm more of a "chip off the ole block" than you'd like to believe. You may not agree with me, but I hope you are proud of me.

I thank you both for instilling in me the incredible values, habits and principles that have molded my business, my decisions, my life. I love you both.

ॐ

What is a Spiritual Entrepreneur?

How do you know if you are one or not? Is this book really for you?

Here's my definition of a Spiritual Entrepreneur:

- They recognize some sort of Supreme Power

- They base their business on values that mean everything to them

- Profit is important but people are even more important

- They love what they do and want to use their gifts and talents to bring joy to themselves and others

- Making a difference in the world is an important part of their life

- Their business is built on high ethics and spiritual principles such as the Law of Attraction

- They are concerned about the planet and contribute to the harmony and well-being of the environment

- A spiritual entrepreneur wants more from their business than just to pay the bills

~ Table of Contents ~

Acknowledgements

I really can't take ownership of this book as I feel that it was written "through" me, not "by" me. Therefore, thanks go first and foremost to a Higher Power who took charge and just got it done.

A huge thank you to my dear friend, Monique Macdonald, who heard about the concept for this book and decided it was a "best seller" from the very beginning. Your belief in me and in this book has been an inspiration!

To Josette Williams, thank you for your constructive feedback and for constantly brainstorming with me. Your support, encouragement and friendship are priceless!

Bobbie Van Riet—your passion for my success has been a huge impetus in my life for many years. You have always seen the best in me. Thank you for discouraging me from writing this book four years ago when I wasn't ready for it and for your encouragement and support in manifesting it so abundantly and clearly now.

Thanks to Cijaye de Pradine who has been a dear friend and supporter of every one of my endeavors since the day we met. Your belief in me has not gone unnoticed or unappreciated.

Karen Learmonth—my incredible photographer who has the beautiful talent and gift of seeing the best in people with and without her camera. Your contribution to my life and this book is so appreciated.

To my special friend Kelly Nault, award winning author, who inspired me to get my book done because of the magnificent job she did on her own. Thank you.

To all the dear friends and clients, Alice Brock, Sandra Lee, Krista Garren, Alfred Pettersen, Barbara Walker, Richard Casavant, Jennifer Maier, Deb Erichsen, Deborah Rubin, Kimberly Easterbrook, Lana Casavant, and Ami Catriona who shared their thoughts and ideas with me and were kind enough to read excerpts and then be honest. Thank you, thank you!

Thanks to Peter Comrie and his amazing partner, Joyce Evans, for their outstanding contribution to the naming of this book. Peter, you've been a great mentor these past few years. Thank you for seeing what you saw in me.

To all of my wonderful clients who over the last few years have inspired me with their commitment and dedication to their success. You have motivated me to want to help entrepreneurs succeed with the greatest joy and ease possible. Thank you for being a huge part of my life.

Thanks to a great editor, Dale McGowan, whose response to the project was so enthusiastic, I couldn't help but want to work with him.

Thank you, Diane Mendez, the most amazing woman on the planet when it comes to fonts and layout of a book. What passion for her work. I did not know that anyone could get so excited about formatting a book until I met Diane. You are truly a gift. For all the late nights you spent and your attention to detail—thank you, thank you!

So much gratitude goes to the team at Animatz who worked with me tirelessly to get the illustrations right. You guys were amazing as you took the vague idea in my head and somehow translated it onto paper. Your patience with my attention to detail was incredible.

To Dan Yeager who created the book cover. I kept on telling him that it was the cover that would sell my book (no pressure of course!) and he came through with flying colors. Dan, my instinct was right on from the moment I saw your work. You're the best. Thank you.

To my sister Julie Railton, and my sister-in-law Kathleen Janzen, thank you for your 'behind the scenes' support. I love you both!

If I have forgotten anyone, please forgive me. I have a whole new appreciation for every author now that I am one. There is lots to think about in this process.

With much love and appreciation to you all,

Jan

Foreword
by Bill Bartmann

I didn't always know the secrets to success in business. I was born on the wrong side of town, I was paralyzed from the waist down at 17 and told I would never walk again, and I was a high school dropout. I was a gang member, a drug addict and an alcoholic. Quite frankly, I was what the world would call a "loser".

There were several things that brought me around to where I am today as a self-made billionaire, a college graduate, a law school graduate and recipient of the National Entrepreneur of the Year Award by Merrill-Lynch, Ernst & Young, NASDAQ, *USA Today*, and *Inc. Magazine,* to name just a few of my accomplishments over the past 40 years.

What created a change from welfare to the 25th richest person in America, from bankrupt to flying my own $25 million dollar jet are precisely the success secrets that Jan talks about in *Devil with a Briefcase*. Success didn't happen overnight in my case and it probably won't happen overnight in yours.

Success is a combination of knowing your values, being in integrity, setting your goals and living with passion. It's about getting along with people, caring about your clients, employees and family. It's about believing in something bigger than yourself.

Jan Janzen has encapsulated her own life experience as a Jehovah's Witness for 38 years and an entrepreneur for more than 25 years in this intriguing and rare book. She's a dynamic businesswoman with plenty of energy combined with a straight shooting style that comes right from the heart. You may not always WANT to hear what she has to say about what it takes to succeed in business, but you will definitely benefit from the truths that she shares with you.

As a member of my own billionaire mentoring program, I know that Jan is driven to succeed and to help others succeed. As a veteran entrepreneur and a minister most of her life, she knows the tools to success in every area of her life and she shares them freely and openly in *Devil with a Briefcase.*

Today, more than ever, entrepreneurs are starting home-based businesses as they feel the economic instability and many of them want more quality time with their family. That's exciting to see. However, most businesses fail, not succeed. Why don't more succeed? Jan's motto that "You don't get what you want in your business, you get who you are" is so true. A solid business plan has to start with who you are as the CEO of your company. Big or small, in whatever part of the world you are in, your business success will be directly linked to your values, your self-esteem and your ability to ride the ups and downs of business.

Even if you know everything there is to know about business, you are going to be pleasantly surprised when you start to read this book. Jan's written about honesty, integrity, choosing your association wisely, being organized, persistent, focused and disciplined with such a different twist, you actually see it from a whole new perspective. The fact that she uses unique stories of her being mobbed in the Andes mountains, how she started speaking publicly at 8 years of age to an audience of over 100 people and why she was willing to carry a No Blood Transfusion card with her at all times, are just some of the fascinating segues into what it takes to be a successful entre-preneur.

I don't care about your religious upbringing. It doesn't matter what you believe about God. Please don't allow any past beliefs about the Jehovah's Witnesses stop you from getting the full impact and benefit from this book! Today Jan is a non-denominational minister for one reason. She wants to help people understand that the way that she was raised—that she was right and everyone else was wrong—is not the happiest and most joyful way to live. For that reason, she is honest and open about the beliefs of the religion that she was an ardent supporter of for most of her life.

In *Devil with a Briefcase,* Jan wants you to get that the Witnesses have a business model and system that works for ANY business and perhaps by understanding the background of a much hated religion, your eyes will be opened to a broader way of thinking about those people who knock on your door on Saturday morning. It's not about being right or wrong, good or bad—it's about knowledge. Pure and simple. Knowledge that can save you a lot of time and money in your business by thinking differently right from the start, and bring you a level of contentment, satisfaction and joy in your business that Jan believes is critical to your long-term success.

If you have been struggling with getting your business off the ground or creating a business that is financially lucrative because of lack of motivation, systems, know-how or a common false belief that you can't be "spiritual" and wealthy, this book will set you straight. There are plenty of "how-to" books out on the market— this book touches your heart and soul so you are inspired and motivated to succeed.

I never thought of myself as a "spiritual entrepreneur" until I understood Jan's definition of what one is and then I got it. Of course, that described me to a tee. I believe there are a lot of spiritual entre-preneurs in the world today who are looking for a home, a community and a way of doing business that is more reflective of a new set of values, and based on a different foundation of ethics. Jan's book, business and ministry will appeal to those of you who resonate with her definition of a spiritual entrepreneur.

The fact that Jan is donating 10% of the sales of the book to micro-financing organizations around the world to help the less fortunate entrepreneurs is typical of Jan's philanthropic philosophy. Not only are you helping your own business by buying this valuable book, you are helping entrepreneurs in developing countries who are faced with struggle, hardship and turmoil in their everyday life. Over the past year, Jan has studied microfinancing thoroughly and is convinced that by helping others through small microfinance loans, we can eradicate poverty.

One of the things that I have gathered in my association with Jan is that she is persistent, she follows through and she walks her talk. Today, that is rare. So it is a pleasure to introduce you, the reader, to an amazing book that will hit you in the head as well as the heart, make you laugh out loud at times, perhaps shake your belief system, open your eyes to the little known secrets of a fascinating religious organization and move you to action in your business.

This book is red hot for a reason. Go find out why for yourself now!

Best wishes,

Bill Bartmann
Author of *Billionaire Secrets to Success*

What the devil does the Devil have to do with business?

Nothing—and *everything*. I grew up with the Devil as a powerful and literal reality. Perhaps the same is true of you. I was raised as a Jehovah's Witness, so the Devil was an integral part of my belief system. Once I made the decision to leave the Jehovah's Witnesses, I jokingly referred to myself as the "devil incarnate," the "excluded," the "outcast."

No longer part of the ranks, I became the Devil with a briefcase. Not the briefcase that I had carried for 38 years of door-to-door ministry as a Jehovah's Witness, but the briefcase of an "out-of-the-box," maverick-thinking entrepreneur and non-denominational minister who no longer viewed having money as undesirable or unspiritual.

I no longer believe in a literal devil that is out to "get me," tempt me, or lead me down the road to sin and perdition. I'd much rather believe that I create my life and that the whole Universe is here to support me to my highest good. But whatever you personally believe, the devil concept is a useful (and fun) one for every entrepreneur. Having some "devilish" qualities is important for a successful entrepreneur.

Why do I say that?

Think about the devil's story for a minute. The devil became the devil when he (or she) stepped out of line, thought for himself, and decided to make up his own rules. He was the first freethinker and entrepreneur. Suddenly there was competition for supremacy in the Garden of Eden! Perhaps this was the true birth of capitalism. Those qualities of thinking outside the box, breaking some rules, thinking for yourself and making decisions that are in line with your values, even though they may be unpopular, are important qualities for the successful entrepreneur.

The trident (or pitchfork) has many associations. Poseidon, the Greek god of the sea, struck the earth with his trident to create earthquakes and subdue storms. In Christian mythology, the trident is a symbol of power associated with the Devil. The Maserati, one of the fastest, raciest, most powerful cars on the market, has a trident in its logo. So the trident is a symbol of power and creativity—two qualities that are vitally important for entrepreneurs today.

Devil with a Briefcase is all about what it takes to be a successful entrepreneur in the 21st century. This is not theory or speculation. The principles outlined are based on principles, habits and systems that I had drilled into me through 38 years as a member of one of the most successful religious organizations in the world. These are principles, habits and systems that I have personally put into practice in over 25 years as an entrepreneur.

This book is not about religion. Promise!

However, looking at my life today as a successful entrepreneur has reaffirmed one fact time and time again. The training, lessons, and values instilled in me as a Jehovah's Witness have stood by me as critical touchstones in how to run a business. Though I don't agree with the dogma of the religion, I will say this: the Jehovah's Witnesses are absolutely brilliant as an organization. Although I left over seven years ago, I still marvel that they take people from all walks of life and train them on a volunteer basis to successfully do what many businesses can't seem to do particularly well with paid help: to successfully sell, to follow a system consistently, to be disciplined and focused, and to duplicate, duplicate, duplicate!

While many people know what the inside of a church looks like or even a local temple, very few people know what the inside of a Kingdom Hall of Jehovah's Witnesses looks like. Even fewer understand the mammoth task this organization accomplishes, publishing books and magazines in 306 languages with almost 100,000 congregations around the world and close to seven million members spending over 1.3 BILLION hours in the dispensing of their religious literature. That's a lot of people spending a lot of time going from door to door!

This book is about looking inside one of the most successful religious organizations in the world to learn vital business lessons from them.

As a coach and mentor to entrepreneurs around the world, I have shared with them many of the tools that have come naturally to me in the business world. Those tools were inculcated in me from childhood by a regimented schedule of public speaking and sales training, learning how to follow a system, and being organized while having a deep passion for my message.

Every lesson I learned in 38 years as a Jehovah's Witness works brilliantly in the business world. The proof is in the pudding. They continue to grow despite an unpopular message. They prosper in almost every country of the world despite major differences in language, culture and lifestyle, and have remained united and consistent. They have overcome severe opposition, outright persecution and constant harassment as an organization and as individuals. I know. During my life in that organization, I had doors slammed in my face, dogs sicced on me, hoses turned on me—and was once mobbed by 100 angry Ecuadorians!

Devil with a Briefcase is a rare glimpse inside the walls of that organization from someone who's been there and knows it intimately. It's a fun book that recounts "tales out of school" and brings home valuable lessons for every entrepreneur. You'll be surprised, even shocked on occasion. You'll laugh and probably shake your head in disbelief at times—but you'll also get some key pointers that will help you grow your business. Whether you are a one-person show or a major corporation wanting to grow your sales team or motivate your staff, this book has something for you.

I write this book with deep respect for a religion that taught me many good lessons in life and in business. Although it is not my spiritual path today, I honor the systems I learned that have made running many businesses over the past 25 years—well, almost easy. I am an entrepreneur at heart and I love the entrepreneurial world. Anything I can do to make your life easier as an entrepreneur, as a business person, or as a company wanting to increase your bottom line while bringing value to your staff, I want to do. This book is a result of the love I have for the business world.

I trust you will enjoy reading it as much as I enjoyed writing it!

Get Organized

Jehovah's Witnesses are probably the best organized organization I know. That may sound redundant—isn't "being organized" what organizations do, after all?

But it isn't. I've seen lots of disorganized organizations. Jehovah's Witnesses, however, isn't one of them.

Jehovah's Witnesses don't just appear out of nowhere on your street on a Saturday morning. They are incredibly well-organized, right down to a little map of your block. A small group will have been assigned that morning to work your street thoroughly. If you are not at home, they take down your house number and note the date on a sheet of paper called a "Not At Home" slip. They note what time of day they called so they can establish your routine in hopes of catching you at home. That's organization.

Are you that organized in your business? Or are you all over the map —cold-calling one day, never following up, and then starting an email campaign the next week before your website is fully functional? Do you have a solid paper trail documenting what you do, or notes scattered all over your office?

Disorganization will cost you precious time and money. Looking for your car keys, searching for that file folder, wondering where the phone number is for a potential client, or even running out of toner in the middle of printing a huge proposal—all of these are signs of disorganization.

I start every day by putting the date at the top of the page in a good old fashioned school exercise book. Every thing that happens that day goes on that page so I can easily find my notes from a particular conversation and my messages.

If you don't have a filing system, a message system, a daytimer or some other record of your appointments, you are NOT organized, and your results will be disastrous. If you are currently suffering from disorganization, you know PRECISELY what I am talking about.

Organization is a habit, just as disorganization is a habit. Choose organization. You will be amazed at how everything in your business is easier and much more fun. If you need help, there is a whole industry called Professional Organizers to help you get started.

Success Secret #2 — Be Willing to Be Different

If everybody seems to be doing it, believing it, or talking about it, so are the vast majority of humans. I call this the "Tribal Mentality." It's tough to leave the tribe. For centuries we have had the message ingrained in us that being part of the tribe is critical to our survival. For a long time, quite frankly, it was. Women were midwives for each other and supported each other through childbirth so they could stay strong as a community. Men got together for barn raisings and plowing fields and came together in tough times. There was a mentality of community that worked.

Today that same "tribal mentality" is not working. Humanity for the most part is caught in a cesspool of poverty thinking, a scarcity mentality, and low self-esteem. They operate from a place of fear, the lowest vibration of energy on the planet.

It is a challenge to leave the tribe and be different. When everybody is in a place of fear, are you willing to see the love? When most people are seeing the lack, do you see the prosperity?

If everybody is jumping off the cliff, are you lining up to jump, too?

I remember my first assembly at school. I was six years old. They were going to sing the National Anthem and I knew that I was going to stand out as being different. My heart raced, my knees knocked, my stomach was queasy. Thirty-nine years later, I still remember that morning assembly vividly. I had been trained from infancy to be different. Here was my first big test, alone without Mom and Dad by my side. As a Jehovah's Witness, I was NOT to sing the National Anthem. I wasn't even to stand for it. That took a lot of courage for a little girl of six. But what it imprinted in my heart and soul like a hot branding iron was that I was willing to be different.

Today, more than ever, we need human beings, entrepreneurs, businesses, small and large corporations to stand out and say, "Let's do this differently. Let's work together in harmony. Let's not ruin the environment for the sake of profit, and let's share with those less fortunate."

Those sentiments are still not mainstream. They are different. But those sentiments also make sense. Are you willing to be different in your business? Yes, your knees may knock, your heart may race and you may even feel a little queasy. But you can do it, and the more of us that are willing to step outside, the greater the impetus that can change the direction this world is heading. This is powerful. I know from experience. I learned it when I was just six years old.

Question to ponder:
When everybody is in a place
of fear, are you willing to see
the love?

Success Secret #3

Be Quiet

Jehovah's Witnesses usually go door-to-door in pairs. One will be the person taking the lead in the conversation; the other will be a back-up or assistant. A critical lesson to learn when being the back-up or assistant is when to be quiet. There is a time to speak and a time (quite frankly) to keep your mouth shut! This quality does not come naturally to many people.

Often when I was the designated leader, I would be leading a person down a line of reasoning, only to have my "silent" partner jump in and take off on a tangent, leading the conversation far afield. There was nothing more frustrating! Any of you who are married or have ever been married know that after a while it becomes a challenge to finish a sentence, never mind an entire story, without having your partner jump in and take over!

Why is it important in business to learn to be quiet? You've probably all heard that once the deal is presented, it is the first person who speaks who loses! I don't like the terms "win" and "lose" in a business deal—if everybody is not winning, it's not a good deal! But the saying makes one thing clear: there is definitely a time to be quiet. Silence is important in business at appropriate times. Learning to be quiet is critical when you are working with a team and work needs to get done. Knowing when to speak and when to be quiet can make or break a sale. Learning to be quiet is also critical when you are listening to a potential partner.

Knowing when to be quiet may be one of the toughest lessons to learn, but it is a valuable one. Learning to be quiet at appropriate times can make you money in business and make you very popular with your clients. Simply knowing when to be quiet can make you stand out as someone who really listens!

"Simply knowing when to be quiet can make you stand out as someone who really listens!"

Success Secret #4	Going from BIG to Workable

I magine looking at the world and knowing that you were responsible for contacting every single person personally. With almost seven billion people on the planet, that would be a monumental task. Yet, as an entrepreneur today, you have that opportunity. In his bestselling book *The World is Flat*, Thomas Friedman clearly shows how globalization has transformed the world of business in the 21st century. But it's one thing to know that such global reach is possible —it can even be exciting to you in business—and quite another to see it as YOUR responsibility. Yet that's exactly how the JWs feel about their task.

The JWs have literally divided and conquered the world organizationally. How can you learn from their example? In other words, how do you go from the BIG picture in your business to something that translates into small daily tasks? I can't think of a better example than the following.

First of all, in most of the larger countries, Jehovah's Witnesses have a Branch Office. That Branch Office reports to the World Headquarters in New York. Each Branch Office is responsible for their country or for a small group of countries. Here in Canada, the Branch Office is in Georgetown, Ontario. That Branch divides the country into Districts—perhaps seven or eight in Canada. Each District has a District Overseer, a man trained by the Headquarters in New York to look after the District. He is responsible for the annual District Convention, as well as the preaching activity and spiritual health of his area.

The District then has several Circuits, each with a Circuit Overseer responsible to the District Overseer and trained by the Branch Office (or occasionally by Headquarters). The Circuit Overseer is responsible for the congregations in his circuit. He must visit each one twice a year and organize a two-day and a one-day annual convention for them. Although the program, the schedule, the theme and all the outlines will be provided by H.Q., he is responsible for assigning each talk to a qualified speaker that he knows from visiting the congregations.

Each congregation in a circuit has a group of men responsible for running the weekly schedule of five meetings per week and over-seeing the spiritual health and welfare of the members. Each congregation is further divided into small book study groups that meet once each week, usually in a member's home. These meetings are typically conducted by one of the men from the group that runs the congregation or by one of the men being groomed for that position that has proved himself trustworthy and knowledgeable.

Those small groups are the very nucleus of what forms the international organization of Jehovah's Witnesses. From those book study groups, all of the preaching work is organized. Each Saturday, for example, they meet in their book study group to prepare before going door-to-door.

Each area that the congregation is assigned to cover geographically is then divided into small maps called territories that are marked literally with every street in an area that can be worked in a reasonable amount of time—usually 2-3 hours. Once assigned a territory map, an individual Witness or the group are personally responsible for reaching every single person that lives in that specified area.

Those maps are checked in and out regularly like a library book and one of the tasks of the circuit overseer is to verify how often those maps are being completed and turned in. That report then goes to the Branch Office which compiles a report for H.Q. so they know where there is a need for more workers. All Jehovah's Witnesses living in the area of a particular congregation attend that congregation—cross-stepping boundaries is frowned upon. You attend the congregation's meetings and preach in the area where you live.

It's an amazing system of taking the globe and breaking it down into workable, bite-sized chunks of territory, delegating the responsibility of running the organization down a chain of command that reports to the next above. No member of any congregation reports to H.Q. or even the Branch Office. They report to their local body of "elders" who go up the chain of command.

Can you utilize a similar system in breaking down your business? Rather than being overwhelmed by the magnitude of the task, can you use a chain of command to get the job done?

Question to ponder:
Rather than being overwhelmed
by the magnitude of the task,
can you use a chain of
command to get the job done?

Did you Know?

The word **entrepreneur** is a French word introduced and first defined by an Irish economist named Richard Cantillon in 1755. According to Cantillon, an entrepreneur is a person who undertakes and operates a new enterprise or venture and assumes some accountability for the inherent risks.

Be a Pioneer

We often think of pioneers as those brave immigrants or settlers who came from foreign countries, braved hardship and settled in new territory. It's a good vision to have in mind when you think about being a pioneer in your area of business.

You've probably heard the saying, "There are those who make things happen, those who watch things happen, and those who say, "What happened!" Which one are you?

A pioneer makes things happen. They are among the first in any field of inquiry, enterprise, or progress. We often use the term today in reference to pioneering medical breakthroughs.

The JWs actually have a group of people within their organization called "pioneers"—people who takes the lead in the preaching work and agree to devote a set number of hours per month and per year in preaching and teaching. I was a pioneer for six years, during which time I agreed to spend 90 hours per month for a total commitment of 1000 hours per year. Although women have a set role in the congregation and are excluded from many responsibilities, both men and women can be pioneers. It is considered a privilege and a responsibility. You are sent to a special training course for two weeks to learn how to be a better teacher, how to organize your time well and how to be a good example for others. The vast majority of pioneers also work part-time to support themselves materially, as there is no financial compensation for being a pioneer. Sometimes the mother or father in a family will be able to pioneer. In my case, both my husband and I were pioneers together for four years.

In business, are you a follower or a leader? Or, heaven forbid, do you fall in the category of "What happened," struggling with emails, blogging, podcasting and webinars. The advantage of being a pioneer is that you get there first. I often use Elance, the top clearinghouse for freelance entrepreneurs, to help me out in my projects. In the seven years since their founding in 1999, Elance has done over $7 billion worth of business.

What's interesting is that Elance does have competition—but you'd never know it. You never hear about them. I only noticed them while on the Elance site—they advertise very discreetly on the top of the Elance web page. But because Elance pioneered the concept, they took first place in the market.

A few years back, I pioneered a novel business concept that combines a home party with pole dancing for everyday women—something that had never been done before. Although I have sold the business, it has gone on to become the number one home pole dancing company in the world. I am a pioneer by nature, and my years as a Jehovah's Witnesses fostered that drive in me to be at the forefront, challenging the odds and stepping where nobody has dared tread before.

Being a pioneer will always have its challenges and obstacles – you don't always know if it will work, you have no role models to follow, you need nerves of steel and it helps to be a visionary. But if being a pioneer is your cup of tea, step into the role fully and embrace the thrills…because there will be plenty of them!

Question to ponder: There are those who make things happen, those who watch things happen, and those who say, "What happened!" Which one are you?

Success *Secret* #6	# Be Visible

D
o you ever have a hard time finding a product, service or company that you wanted? Does that frustrate you? Sure it does —your time is precious, and with today's fast-paced technology and access to a plethora of information, we don't tolerate delay in getting information.

So how visible are you? I learned to be visible from an early age as I stood on street corners holding *Watchtowers* and *Awakes* with my Mom or Dad. The lesson I learned was that one method of exposure wasn't enough. Not everybody is at home when JWs call, so they need to reach people as many ways as possible. Because they believe that lives are at stake—theirs and yours—they make a concerted effort to reach you through various means.

Anyone visiting New York will notice Trump Towers, but the headquarters of Jehovah's Witnesses is also large and impressive. And right across the top of one of the buildings, in massive letters, are the words READ GOD'S WORD THE HOLY BIBLE DAILY. They are proud of their message and they make it visible.

How visible is your business? Do you have a web presence? Are you in the yellow pages, if appropriate? Is the name of your company clearly marked on the building? Is the address clear and prominent? Do you have business cards with all of the appropriate information? Are your brochures prominently displayed at a networking event with a stand-up display OR are they laying flat on the table like everyone else's?

When I owned a pole dancing business, we designed a doll on a pole stand for our business owners. At the base of the pole was a place for their business cards. It drew a lot of attention because it was visible and different. It wasn't just another sheet of paper, flyer, business card or brochure like the rest. It was highly visible!

Drive past many florists or pizza places and you'll see people dressed up in sandwich boards or costumes, drawing attention to their business. Granted, many of them are a poor testimony to the business, standing depressed and soggy in the rain, waving a banner, but still—it creates visibility for the business.

If *you* didn't know *you*, how easy would you be to find? Look at all the ways that people can find you, every avenue of visibility through which you are now exposing your business to traffic, online and offline, and ensure that you are visible.

Be Persistent

J ehovah's Witnesses are persistent. As I'm sure you've noticed, they don't give up easily. They will try you in the morning, in the afternoon, in the evening and on the weekend, until they get you at home. In areas where there is a high ratio of Jehovah's Witnesses to the population (yes, they know all of those statistics, too), they will even turn over those persistent not-at-homes identified by the "Not At Home" slips to someone else in the congregation or a full-time minister with a quota of preaching time to meet each month, and that person will either phone or write a letter. They are *determined* to reach you.

How persistent are you? Do you give up easily, or do you follow the chase? Do you try to reach people at different times? Are you creative in the methods that you use to connect with people? If you can't reach the manager of a business on the phone, do you drop in with a flyer and business card? If an email doesn't work, do you pick up the phone?

We all know how persistent some of the Internet marketing gurus are. Some of them will market every day. They are creative in their approach, but most importantly, they are persistent. They don't give up until you either say YES or unsubscribe.

People today give up far too easily. A few rejections, a few objections, a hot day, a rainy day, a phone call not returned, a client canceling an appointment, and they're done. Defeated.

Persistence means persevering, continuing, repeating. That means you just keep on going. Next time you feel like giving up, remember that Jehovah's Witness who knocked on your door on a rainy, cold Saturday morning – and decide right then and there that you can be just as persistent, if not more so, in your business!

"Persistence means persevering, continuing, repeating. That means you just keep on going."

Success	
Secret	# Turning a Negative
#8	# into a Positive

I remember doing a major presentation of a technology called On-Time that I was selling to the automotive industry. The device would literally shut down a car if a person with bad credit did not make their payments on time. So I had my laptop loaded with the software and my model Hummer loaded with the device. I had practiced going through it beforehand, but in the middle of this very important presentation, everything crashed. I turned to the owner of the dealership and said, "Well it's a good thing our technology is better and more reliable than Sony's." He laughed. I rebooted and this time the laptop came through for me. He placed a large order and became one of my best customers.

As a Jehovah's Witness, I learned to turn negatives into positives all the time. I guess when you are surrounded by a negative reaction to your message most of the time, you learn to either sink or swim. Even when there is a war, a murder, or some other tragedy, Jehovah's Witnesses see it as the fulfillment of Bible prophecy—and for them, that's a good thing!

You may remember when we had the Tylenol™ tampering disaster several years ago that took the lives of seven people. I'm sure the drug company that makes Tylenol™ had a few sleepless nights over that one—but they made the necessary changes by inventing the tamper-proof packaging that is now the industry standard. They took a horribly negative situation and came back with a positive message, returning Tylenol™ to best-seller status for Johnson and Johnson in a relatively short time.

Negative stuff will happen in your business. It's inevitable. Projects that didn't go right. Customers who don't like you. Competition that bad-mouths you. Bad media coverage! How you react will determine your success. If you run and hide every time something negative happens, you will spend a lot of time hiding! Learn to turn it into a positive.

"If you run and hide every time something negative happens, you will spend a lot of time hiding!"

Tune in to Your Market

How tuned in are you to your market? Let's say that you have a product or service to market to moms. Do you know what moms want? Have you listened to their needs? Do you honor their time constraints, their need for easy facilitation of processes and specific information? When she comes home from work at 6:00 with two hungry children to feed, a husband out-of-town on business and a dog that hasn't seen anyone all day, what does mom need? A jar that only a man can open, a package with hard-to-read instructions, a complicated recipe with foreign-sounding ingredients? Hardly.

So have you really sat down to figure out what your market wants, needs, and will pay for? Do you know how they want to receive that information? How much, what time, how long? Do you know what repels them and what appeals?

The covers of the JW magazines, the *Watchtower* and *Awake*, are actually different for every market. For the magazine distributed to a predominately white population, the pictures will be of white people. For magazines distributed in Africa for example, the pictures will be of dark-skinned people. Why? Because people can relate best to what they know. They don't want to come across as a "white" organization—JWs are an international organization, and with that distinction comes certain marketing challenges and responsibilities. They tune into their markets and resonate with them.

Do you tune into your market and adjust appropriately, or is your presentation a one-size-fits-all?

Some savvy entrepreneurs will take a presentation and market it to a niche market with 95% of the same information but a look tailored to the market in question. If you are teaching patient retention skills to chiropractors, are those skills truly all that different from those for massage therapists, dentists or naturopaths? So a smart entrepreneur may change 5% of the information, the cover of the handout, the first slide of the power point presentation and the facts regarding patient retention in that industry and be able to focus on an entirely new market. Brilliant? Absolutely! Learn to do that and you will have an amazing business!

Question to Ponder:

Do you tune into your market and adjust appropriately, or is your presentation a one-size-fits-all?

Success Secret #10

Using Volunteers

Do you feel like you need to have paid and salaried employees to make your business work? Do you think that people won't help you unless you have the money to pay them? Think again!

Do you realize that the entire organization of Jehovah's Witnesses is run by volunteers? NOT ONE person is paid for their work. NOT ONE. Not one person going from door-to-door, not one missionary, not one elder in the congregation, not one person working at the headquarters receives monetary compensation for their work. NOT ONE! Every single person is a volunteer, all seven million of them.

Do you understand the implications of this statement? A small percentage who are full time volunteers at a branch office or the headquarters or missionaries in a foreign land receive a very small monthly stipend to cover personal expenses. That's quite a feat to run an organization of this magnitude with nothing but volunteers, don't you think?

So if you believe that you need money to start hiring people, you may be incorrect. One of my business colleagues put on a hiring seminar and brought in top notch businessmen who had retired from their own businesses. They agreed to work for him for a period of one to five years with no monetary compensation. Why?

That's the secret in both cases.

People will follow a leader with a strong vision and passion who conveys a powerful message. People who buy into a purpose and passion will do amazing things. Finding volunteers is not the answer for every business, but for many organizations, utilizing the power of volunteers is absolutely perfect.

"If you believe that you need money to start hiring people, you may be incorrect."

Success Secret #11

On Top of Technology

Blogs, RSS feeds, Direct to Desktop, Social Bookmarking—technology can be an overwhelming experience. But technology is here to stay, so those of you who think that having an email address at hotmail is good enough—please get your head out of the sand and get going!

I don't enjoy discussing technology any more than many of you, but I do love what it can do for my business. Blogs, podcasts, the Internet, and video emails are just the tip of the iceberg when it comes to technology. You think it's amazing today? I promise you that in ten years we'll look back at how we are communicating now and laugh. Do you realize that the whole technology scenario really only became mainstream less than ten years ago? I bet that fewer than 1% of you had an email address ten years ago! Technology is changing and improving and growing—and you need to get with the program!

In 1914, the first president of the JWs produced the *Photo Drama of Creation*. It was a film and slide presentation with pictures synchronized to a sound recording—a pioneer to the modern movie. It was considered well ahead of its time and was eventually seen by hundreds of thousands.

JWs used radio extensively in the 1920s and 30s, using hundreds of radio stations to broadcast Bible lectures. The use of the radio was eventually eclipsed by increased house-to-house visits, complete with portable phonographs and recorded Bible talks. They would literally show up at a house with a portable phonograph and start playing when you opened the door! Again they were way ahead of their time technologically.

Where are you with technology? Are you feeling overwhelmed or excited? Those two words are opposite sides of the same coin. Which one will you choose?

Success Secret #12   Accept Correction

It's a tough thing to be told you're wrong. Many people immediately go into a defensive mode, listing all of the reasons they did or didn't do something. They can't bear to accept the repercussions of being wrong. And worse yet, they hate being told what they did wrong!

Everybody makes mistakes. The best of the best have failed, picked themselves up and started again. Robert Kiyosaki, best-selling author of *Rich Dad, Poor Dad*, notes that his rich father severely chastised him at times for foolishness in business. Robert accepted the blame and moved on to building a multi-million dollar business.

Many things will stop us from accepting correction. Mostly it's pride and an errant belief that it is wrong to make a mistake. We have perhaps been berated in an unloving way and so anything that resembles a "correction" we find humiliating and uncomfortable.

The JWs believe that correction is an indication of love, that someone actually cares enough to tell you what you are doing wrong. I know, having been on both the receiving and giving ends of correction, that it's much easier to receive correction than give it. It can be a tough call to let someone know that they did something wrong. It's much easier to avoid it and let it ride. But allowing someone to remain in error is not the most loving course of action. So when someone has the courage and the consideration to give you correction, rather than go into defensive mode, start off by saying, "Thank you for sharing your viewpoint with me. I will definitely give it some consideration."

The words may sting at the moment, but those will be some of your finest lessons in life and in business.

A businessman recently corrected me in front of another person. I was taken aback, shocked and hurt. However, I thanked him and went away to think about it. He was absolutely right, and I appreciated that he cared enough about me to correct me. I admit—it took me a few days to unruffle the feathers he had ruffled and to soothe the hurt and pain his correction brought up in me, but in looking back, I am truly grateful.

Accepting correction was a part of my growing up as a JW. It's a part of life that I don't relish, but I do cherish.

Question to Ponder:

Can you see correction as

an indication that someone

cares about you enough to

share something uncomfortable

with you?

Success	
Secret	# Be in Integrity
#13	

Integrity is defined as adherence to moral and ethical principles, soundness of moral character, honesty. Being in integrity is easy to say but at times quite difficult to do.

I remember learning that if a cashier gave me the wrong change, I needed to tell her. My income tax was done accurately every year. I wouldn't have dreamed of renting a movie containing adult content. I never read a horoscope or even knew my astrological sign. My skirts were never above my knees and my tops were never cut too low. Why not? Because every one of those things would have been out of integrity with Bible principles and with the strong religious dogma of the JWs that had been drilled into my head for 38 years.

Integrity in business can be a mixed blessing. It's easy to have a mission or vision statement that is overflowing with great words like integrity, values, honesty and commitment, but it can be a challenge to live up to those ideals where the rubber meets the road. Are you in integrity, even in the little things?

I notice when an entrepreneur says they will get back to me on a certain date and they don't. I take note when a business claims to be meticulous about customer service but their receptionist doesn't say thank you as she puts me on hold and doesn't come back for ten minutes. It stands out when a company sends me marketing material and then doesn't answer my email when I have a question.

That's being out of integrity. Are you in integrity in your business, even when it is inconvenient or may cost you money? When you say something, do you follow through? We'll all be out of integrity once in awhile; we're all human. But when you are, do you notice it, or do you gloss over it? Do you make amends and do whatever it takes to compensate for your error?

Integrity is a powerful word. It means more than just being honest. Integrity denotes a strong adherence to ethical principles and values. One thing I definitely learned growing up was to know those principles and values so clearly, so perfectly, so thoroughly, that being in integrity was second nature. Can you know that so clearly in your own business?

Question to Ponder:

Are you in integrity in your

business, even when it is

inconvenient or may cost

you money?

Success Secret #14

Stop Caring So Much About What Other People Think About You

We live in a world that preaches personal freedom but then obsesses about what everybody else is doing or NOT doing. I hate having to wait in a grocery store checkout line because I am nauseated by the ridiculous amount of literature printed about celebrities. Do you care who's pregnant, who's having an affair, and who has just lost or gained 30 pounds? I sure don't. I'd be much more interested in the tremendous amount of good news out there – about the children making a difference, the phenomenal philanthropy that is happening, and some positive information to stimulate my thinking.

Here are some potentially tough questions for you. Do you hate controversy? Do you think that there is something wrong with you if not everyone likes you? Do you cower if someone questions your point of view?

A successful entrepreneur learns to face the opposition and definitely needs to get over the concept that EVERYBODY will like you or agree with you. They won't! I always say that there are people who don't like Oprah Winfrey or Mother Teresa—so I don't have a hope in hell everyone will like me! So seriously, get over it.

It has surely been easier for me to take this point of view because opposition is such a regular occurrence in the life of any JW. You can't have such radically different viewpoints, be as visible as they are, go completely against mainstream ideas, proclaim your views to the world and not have opposition. It's impossible.

As a matter of fact, I was told that if people liked me, then I must not be following Jesus closely enough. After all, they hated him enough to kill him! How's that for a line of reasoning? So being disliked, persecuted, and ostracized was a good thing in my life for all those years.

My only question today is this: What do I think about how I lived my life today, the people I helped, the thoughts I thought, the challenges I handled and the love that I spread a little bit further? If I can go to bed and sleep like a baby, then all is well in my world.

You and I are not going to have the whole world like us! So why not just get over that idea and get on with life? Do *you* like *you*? That is probably the biggest question of all time. That is where I start every day. Do I like me today? I'll be honest—some days I like myself more than other days. But some people will never be happy with you no matter what you do, so why go through life trying to keep anyone else happy—except yourself?

Of course we want everyone to like us. But I have found that the clearer you are in your conviction, the surer you are of your beliefs, intentions, goals and vision, the more that supportive people will be attracted to you and unsupportive people will be repelled. Lao-Tzu wrote, "When you are content to be simply yourself and don't compare or compete, everybody will respect you." Notice he didn't say, "everybody will *like* you."

JWs are definitely not liked by the vast majority of the world, but many people—even those who do not like them—respect them for their courage, conviction and willingness to stick to their values and beliefs, even under pressure.

Today, many people, entrepreneurs, businesses, and politicians waffle in their statements, viewpoints, and beliefs because they are always trying to please everybody. It creates confusion, chaos, lies, and lack of integrity. When you stick to your guns, despite opposition, people may not like you, but they will often respect you. But most of all, you will respect yourself!

Success Secret #15

Make Yourself Available in More Languages

$\mathbf{A}$re you in a niche market that you feel is shrinking? Do you feel like you have explored every avenue in your own market? What about the rest of the world?

Have you ever heard of Kabyle, Altay or Bassa? You are probably wondering whether they are cities, countries, a new clothing designer, or new herbs for weight loss! Keep guessing. In case you are ever playing Trivial Pursuit, Kabyle is a language spoken by more than 3 million people, primarily in Algeria. Altay is the official language of the Altai Republic in Russia, and Bassa is a language spoken in Cameroon.

The JW organization publishes literature in 306 languages, including Kabyle, Altay and Bassa. There's a lesson here for every business and entrepreneur. For example, this book will be available in many languages. English, believe it or not, is **not** the most widely spoken language (that would be Mandarin Chinese). English may be the international language of business, but having learned two other languages fluently, I know that my preferred language to LEARN in is English. In other words, every person most likely wants to learn what you have to teach in his or her mother tongue, whether or not they speak English. So if you are only making your information available in English, you are missing out on a massive market potential.

If you are feeling limited in any way by your market – just pick one more language and have everything translated into it and you have potentially doubled or tripled your market. The limitation is only in your head. Today with technology, translation into other languages is not difficult, nor necessarily expensive. And the benefits could be absolutely phenomenal.

'Le Diablo con un maletin'

'La diablette et sa serviette'

सैथान अटाची के सात

Success Secret #16

Be Passionate

Being passionate about your business is considered a necessity by some and a luxury by others. However, everything I read and study about successful entrepreneurs is that passion is more valuable than skill set, knowledge, or talent. One of my business mentors used to say to me, "Passion on fire is more valuable than knowledge on ice."

So how passionate are you?

Perhaps you think of passion only in a romantic sense. Being passionate about someone drives people to do some pretty wild and crazy things. We've all heard about men broadcasting proposals of marriage on billboards, a message pulled by a plane across the sky, a proposal exchanged between skydivers as they plummet to earth. One of my friends had her diamond engagement ring brought to her by a porpoise as she and her sweetheart swam with them in the Caribbean. We may shake our head and say, "But that's different. That's love— this is business."

Is that so?

The most successful entrepreneurs I know eat, breathe, sleep, and LOVE their business. Bill Gates, Warren Buffet, Donald Trump, Richard Branson, Martha Stewart, Bill Bartmann, or Oprah Winfrey could all quit their jobs tomorrow and live a pretty amazing life, don't you think? What drives them to continue on for one more season, one more real estate deal, or one more company launch? It's passion.

I believe that passion is a symptom. Just as much as my friend's romantic engagement proposal was a symptom of many months of courting and a strong relationship built on trust and love, passion in your business is the result of doing many of the things that I talk about in this book. You don't buy passion in the third aisle, second shelf of the Personal Development section of the department store. It comes from using your talents, knowing your gifts, having a clear and strong vision, a deep commitment, an action plan in place, and faith, hope and trust in your life.

The recipe for success in any business unequivocally MUST include passion. It's what drives the best of the best in the business world. Ask yourself: On a scale of 1 to 10, where is your passion for your business? If it's not a 10, ask yourself why not. It's worth stopping right here and getting your passion up there, red hot and rarin' to go!

"The recipe for success in any business unequivocally MUST include passion."

Success Secret #17

Be Honest

We live in a world of dishonesty. It's so prevalent that we can forget what honesty is. We've all had experiences with business people or corporations that are unscrupulous, unethical or use questionable practices. Being raised by parents who spoke German, we used the word *scheister* (or shyster) to describe someone who was underhanded or dishonest. It's still the word that comes to mind and has a good feel for what I am describing.

I was raised to be honest—no ifs, ands or buts. It didn't matter how much you suffered for your honesty; you were expected to be honest. As a result, Jehovah's Witnesses today are often entrusted with responsibility simply because of their religious association rather than proof of trustworthiness as a personal characteristic. They are known around the world for their honest stand, so just by association they are labeled as honest. That's a huge compliment.

In business, once you have the reputation of being honest, you will go far. You would do well to guard it as a precious possession. A businesswoman and I once had a "falling out," as her style of doing business wasn't in line with my principles. However, what was most fascinating was that a few weeks later, she came back to me and said: "I know you were completely honest with me about the past situation. It hurt, but you were right. I now know you will tell me the truth, even when it's hard for you. So now I need someone to tell me the truth about this situation I am facing. I know I can trust you to do that for me." And we're back to doing business together again.

Finding an honest person is so rare today that people are actually skeptical of honesty when they encounter it. Will you *really* do what you say? Do you *really* mean what you promised? Will you *really* honor the price? Are you open about your policies, or is there a lot of "fine print"?

Your honesty in business will be under scrutiny 24/7. People will oftentimes be looking for you to fail, to slip up or to catch you in a lie. And at some point in time, you probably will, even inadvertently. But if you are honest even about your mistakes, errors, and failures, you will gain back the respect—sometimes tenfold—by being honest.

This seems so simple. Be honest. However, I know that saying it and living it are two very different things. How honest are you?

"Guard your reputation
for being honest as a
prized possession."

Build Relationships

We hear this all the time today in the business world. It's all about relationships, build relationships, create relationships, and develop relationships. And it's absolutely true. The problem is many people don't know how to build relationships. You know we need some help in relationship-building when you hear that over 50% of marriages end in divorce!

What is the foundation of any good personal relationship? Communication, trust, friendship, honesty, integrity, similarity of values, and accountability, to name just a few. So which of those personal standards hold true in building your business relationships?

There is no difference—there really isn't. So every single quality that applies in your personal relationship applies in your business relationships. If you look at your business relationships with the same value as your personal relationships, your business can only prosper. You will stand out in the crowd, because people talk about building relationships but rarely do.

Relationship-building is a two-way street. It's about talking, yes, but it's also about listening. What are your clients' concerns, what are their pains, what keeps them awake at night? You don't want to know this just because they will make you money, but because you are interested in building a relationship.

Not every personal relationship will be perfectly suited to you, and the same is true for business relationships. But I learned from banging on stranger's doors for tens of thousands of hours, looking for a listening ear, that building relationships takes time, perseverance, effort and patience. In some places, Jehovah's Witnesses return for another visit if they just get a smile from you. They really work hard to develop a relationship with you because they believe you are important.

That's a good place to start in building your own relationships. Witnesses knock on doors at all hours of the day and in all kinds of weather. They are *committed* to relationship-building.

How committed are you? Are you going through continual "business divorce"? Are you shooting yourself in the foot because as strong as your marketing message is, your method of handling customer complaints stinks, or your front receptionist sounds like sour grapes? Examine your relationship-building process from start to finish and find the weak spots because your relationships are only as strong as the weakest link in the chain that builds them.

"Building relationships

takes time, perseverance,

effort and patience."

Success Secret #19   The Power of Education

A man who consults to some very powerful people around the world held a teleclass in which he stressed the need to educate your prospective clients. He talked about the qualification process you need to bring your prospective clients through, each and every time. That means that they need to be pre-interested, pre-motivated, pre-qualified and predisposed. When you have clients finally reaching you after they have been through this four-step process, the sale is much more secure. How did this marketing guru recommend that you get someone through these four steps? Through the power of education.

People only know how to buy on price. You need to educate them so they can base their decision on knowledge. Entrepreneurs go for the jugular in relationships all the time. They expect someone they just met to marry them. Possible—but highly unlikely. Most people need to learn about you, decide if they like you, feel good about all the interactions with you and go slowly. Start dating before you sleep together! One night stands are just that—one-nighters. You don't want that in your business.

Have a process through which people can learn about you and your company. It may be a monthly newsletter, a 24/7 audio recording that is available, a consumer guide that you have written about your industry, a teleclass that informs and educates or a brochure, pamphlet or book. In many ways, this book is a way to educate people so they can decide whether they like Jan Janzen and want to do further business with me.

Not everybody buys a book from a JW right out of the gate. They may start out by having an interesting conversation in which they learn something or get a question answered. The next time they accept a small tract, a brochure or a magazine. The Witnesses are avid proponents of education. It's why they spend as much time as they do on their own education. If education is going to be a way of life for JWs—and it is, once you become one—then they are pre-qualifying their potential candidates through an educational process. If you don't like to learn, hate reading, and can't sit still for an hour or two at a meeting, you won't like being a JW! By reaching you through the very same process that they expect you to follow, they are educating you right from the get-go.

Harvard president Derek Bok once said, **"If you think education is expensive, try ignorance."**

Education is the lifeblood of any successful business. Every successful entrepreneur I have met spends thousands of dollars, sometimes hundreds of thousands of dollars on their education. Get yourself educated and educate your clients. Ignorance, the opposite of education, is way too high a price to pay!

Question to Ponder:
Do you have a process through
which people can learn about
you and your company?

Success Secret #20

Don't Think a Spiritual Person is a Doormat

O ne of the most common misconceptions I see in the spiritual entrepreneurs I coach is this belief that you always have to be "nice" or you aren't a conscious or spiritual business person. As more and more emphasis is put on customer service, client retention, and 100% unconditional guarantees, you may not know where to set your boundaries in business.

This, understandably, is a delicate issue. When is enough enough? In my *Heart to Heart Selling* CD, I teach that we come across people who will never be satisfied. There are some people who will nitpick and find fault even if we give them our best price, our best service and our finest product. They are miserable through and through, and all the good customer service is not going to change that fact. They are the ones who make your life miserable. So do you lie down and ask them to drive over you one more time so you can really feel rotten and get beaten up again? Trust me, those people will probably speak badly about you no matter what you do. Sometimes being firm with them is the most respectful and best way of dealing with them.

I learned this lesson one day, in a small village 10,000 feet above sea level in the mountains of Ecuador. Several of us had just arrived in the village to begin preaching. It was a few days before Christmas. We didn't realize that the village priest was giving his Christmas sermon just as we arrived. I started going from door-to-door with some of the local women from the congregation while the rest of the group, the men, started at the other end of the village. About thirty minutes in, we rounded a corner and literally faced an angry mob of about 100 Ecuadorian Catholics. A close female friend of the priest rushed out of the crowd and pushed me in the chest shouting, "Get her, she's the one!" I had lived in the country long enough to know that this was a serious situation. In that instant, I had to decide how to react. My safety and the safety of my companions was at stake.

Instinctively, I raised my right hand and put my index finger in her face. I looked her straight in the eye and said, in a calm but menacing tone of voice, "Don't you dare touch me again." I then took a step backwards and said to the crowd in a loud voice, "Do not bother us. We are leaving your village immediately." We turned and walked down the path, and although they harassed a few of the women by stealing their book bags, no one touched me, and we left the village virtually unharmed. We did press charges, as this was not the first time we had been assaulted, and the courts ruled in our favor.

I learned that day that sometimes being nice is not the answer. Firmness, fearlessness and a "don't mess with me" attitude is sometimes necessary. I've had to use it once or twice in business— and though it is never my first, second or even third choice of conduct, I remember that, according to the scriptures, even Jesus lost his cool a few times when necessary. He walked into the temple and overturned the tables of the money changers, for example. Being a spiritual and socially responsible business person does not mean that you are a doormat for the world to walk on.

Success Secret #21

Defend Your Rights

B ecause of the common belief that a God-fearing person will be a doormat, many people assume Jehovah's Witnesses must be pushovers. That is one of the most common misconceptions about JWs. You probably don't realize that some of your freedoms are yours to enjoy because of the legal battles that Jehovah's Witnesses have fought and won, for themselves and for you. Constitutions have been changed because of their legal battles all over the world.

During the 1930s and 1940s, many JWs were arrested for their preaching work, and court cases were fought in the interest of preserving our freedom of speech, press, assembly, and worship. In the United States, appeals from lower courts resulted in the Witnesses winning 43 cases before the Supreme Court of the United States. Favorable judgments have also been obtained from high courts in other lands. Concerning these court victories, Professor C. S. Braden, in his book *These Also Believe*, said of the Witnesses:

> They have performed a signal service to democracy by their fight to preserve their civil rights, for in their struggle they have done much to secure those rights for every minority group in America. When the civil rights of any one group are invaded, the rights of no other group are safe. They have therefore made a definite contribution to the preservation of some of the most precious things in our democracy.

As an entrepreneur or corporation, there will be times when you need to defend your rights. It may be going after a payment that is not forthcoming from a client; it may be defending your name because of slander or public defamation of character; or it may be to defend a trademark or copyright issue.

Just because you are a "nice guy" in business doesn't make you an automatic pushover. If you think that to succeed, you need to roll over and play dead, think again. According to Professor Braden, some of your rights have been protected by an organization that preaches love, humility and obedience yet has the backbone to take on governments when they stand in the way of doing what that organization believes is right. Pick your battles carefully, but don't be afraid to defend your rights. Doing so is, in itself, your right!

"Just because you are a 'nice guy' in business doesn't make you an automatic pushover."

Success Secret #22

Note the Details

As a Jehovah's Witness walks up to your door, they are looking at your yard, your car, your garden, the appearance of your house and any evidence of children. As you open the door, they are noticing whether or not you look busy, harried, angry, bewildered or delighted to see them. (Yes, some people are delighted!) As they speak with you, they are noticing at what points you ask questions, what you disagree with, what views you share, and every detail of your body language. They are trained to be very observant.

After they leave your home, they will take notes about your conversation, any scriptures read, any objections you raised and poignant comments discussed. They will note what they agreed to do, whether they are to come back with an answer, bring a specific piece of literature, or return with someone more knowledgeable in a given area—or whether it is best that they not ever call again! They are fanatical about details.

One thing that I see missing with many entrepreneurs and businesses is attention to the details. I remember visiting a spa with my sister. It was her treat and I was thrilled for us to have the day being pampered in luxury. However, the person responsible for my well-being and care that day did not tell me her name. I was left wondering who she was and what her role was. We were never asked what we wanted to do about lunch, so we sat side by side with our feet in sudsy water, our stomachs growling, wondering what to do about lunch. Finally we asked, and they ordered in for us from the restaurant next door. Eating my Greek salad would have felt much more like pampering if those small details had been looked after meticulously.

The details make the difference. The other day I took my car in for servicing. As I pulled in under the covered bay area (a godsend here in rainy Vancouver), a young woman came right to my door and said, "Good morning, Miss Janzen, may I take your car for you? They are waiting inside for you." Wow—from a car dealership! I was impressed. She's probably making minimum wage, but she made an impression on me and the company made an impression on me for their attention to detail. I could have parked the car, opened the door myself and gone in to figure out what to do next. But their fastidious attention to detail was noteworthy.

Look at the details in your business—right from the impression of your website to the spelling in your newsletters to the way your voicemail message is clear and professional. If you think that people aren't noticing the details—trust me, they are.

Question to Ponder:
How much attention do
you pay to the details in
your business?

Discipline

Many entrepreneurs lack discipline. We don't really like that word, but in disregarding it, we often disregard its meaning and application in our life as well. The dictionary defines "discipline" in many ways. Discipline can be an activity, exercise, or a regimen that develops or improves a skill—training, or a set or system of rules and regulations. If you want to grow and develop your business, you need discipline in all of its forms.

Why do many entrepreneurs hate the word or thought of discipline? Perhaps the answer lies in the nature of entrepreneurship. So many of us became entrepreneurs because following the rules, staying the course, and listening to others was unappealing at best—or because freedom is our middle name!

What unfortunately happens is that many entrepreneurs don't realize that it is discipline that will give you the freedom to enjoy life and your business. If you are flying by the seat of your pants with no set discipline, you will be headed for financial and business ruin! If that sounds harsh, let me tell you—not having any discipline in your life is even harsher, because being broke is about as far from freedom as you can get!

Discipline is an activity that develops or improves a skill. If you want to become a better business person, there are skills that you probably need to improve. Perhaps team building, accounting, marketing or sales are skills that need improving if you are going to take your business to the next level. It is that set or system of rules and regulations that will give you much needed parameters for your business and give any employees, subcontractors, and even clients a guideline as to how you do business.

Discipline is actually a great quality to develop as an entrepreneur. Of all the things I am grateful for from my training as a JW, learning the value of discipline is far and away the greatest lesson. "Disciplined" is a word that the majority of my friends, colleagues and business associates would use to describe me. It comes naturally today after decades of daily training.

Being disciplined in your business is a godsend. It really is. Look at how disciplined you are in your business and see where you can improve or cultivate more discipline in your life.

"It is discipline that will give you the freedom to enjoy life and your business."

Use Stories

Facts tell, stories sell. Are you using stories to grow your business? Many entrepreneurs feel uncomfortable telling stories for some reason, but successful marketing is all about stories. I'm telling you a story right now, while educating you in business.

Why should you use stories? People can relate to stories. They can't necessarily relate to the concept of being obedient, but anyone who reads the biblical story of Noah and the flood gets the importance of obedience. You may not understand the importance of honesty until you read the story of the liar who was struck with leprosy. The Bible is full of stories, and I grew up with stories as an integral part of my learning process. I will never forget the ramifications of Dinah's friendship with the pagans—she got raped, a lot of people were murdered and she brought shame on her whole nation. To a young mind, that story is a pretty powerful incentive to choose one's friends carefully. Right or wrong, good or bad, it shows the power of stories.

Many years ago, as I started to market Jan Janzen to the world, I decided I would tell my story of leaving the Jehovah's Witnesses after 38 years and the repercussions of such a decision. It is a story that has inspired many people and fascinated thousands more. It's a story told with a purpose, an intent, a reason. Many people feel like they are trapped by a religion, marriage, culture, business, or economic situation that they don't want to be in, but don't know that they can leave or do anything about it. It feels too serious, too threatening to move out and onwards in their life. My story has given many people courage to do what they really needed to do.

Can you use stories in your business more? How can you use stories to increase your marketing impact?

We all liked bedtime stories. They are soothing, comforting, and build trust. Today, the world is riveted by reality TV shows, which are real life stories. The magazines are full of stories of celebrities and their latest shenanigans! So people obviously love stories.

I can recite a thousand Bible stories drilled into me from infancy down to the last detail, even though I may not have looked at them for years. Why? Because they were used powerfully to drive home lessons, teach principles and instill strong values in me. I bet you have some good stories. Why not use them in your business to inspire and motivate people to action?

"Facts tell, stories sell.
Are you using stories to
grow your business?"

Focus

I n Donald Trump and Robert Kiyosaki's book, *Why We Want You to Be Rich*, Robert gives the best acronym for FOCUS: **Follow One Course Until Success.**

Since the late 1800s, the JWs have believed in the coming of the "end of the world." This refers not to the actual planet but to the elimination of all wrongdoing, bad people and wicked systems, to use their terminology. The end of the world has been predicted more than once—1914 and 1975, to be exact—but still hasn't come. Yet they remain focused on their goal—eternal life in a Paradise Earth.

I learned focus as a child. I never thought that I would get to school, never thought I would graduate from high school, never believed I would get married and certainly would never see the year 2000. I lived my life focused on doing what I was told was required to live in that Paradise Earth. That meant not going to University and not pursuing a full-time job. I was even encouraged to not have children or buy a house so that my life could be more focused on my religious activities. I was like a race horse with blinders on—my goal— PARADISE!

It may seem far-fetched or amazing that I would, (along with millions of other devotees) give up so many personal desires in pursuit of something as elusive as paradise, but it didn't feel elusive to me at any time. It was a focus that was so instilled in me that I didn't even realize my peripheral vision was completely obliterated. I knew the truest meaning of focus. Today I practice that in my business. When I set my mind to something, watch out!

Part of the reason businesses fail is that people are all over the map. They are off on this tangent, then another, then another, until there are a dozen unrelated things on their plate—and nothing is accomplished. Focus is what a magnifying glass will do to a piece of paper when it catches the sun's ray and harnesses the energy of it. It will literally start a fire!

You can't be all things to all people—not in today's information-driven world. You really need to focus and stick to that course until successful. Don't deviate and don't get distracted. Stay true to your course and put those blinders on.

There will always be naysayers, people who tell you it can't be done—but you have to have incredible focus to succeed. I no longer believe the end of the world is coming (not in my lifetime, at least), but I live my life with a focus that is as clear and sharp as it was for those 38 years when I did. I am still a woman on a mission, and focus is my middle name! Are you that focused? Follow One Course Until Success and you will be amazed at what happens in your life!

Devil With A Briefcase

Success Secret #26

Speak Up

Just as there are times to be quiet, there are times to speak up. King Solomon, one of the wisest men who ever lived, actually said, "There is a time to keep quiet and a time to speak."

As an entrepreneur, when do you speak up? If you are doing a sales presentation, speak up. When asked what you do for work, speak up. When your rights are being bulldozed, speak up!

That said, you probably speak more than you need to or even should.

Many words are wasted, and women can be more guilty of this than men. We speak about three times more than men! I know there are lots of jokes out there about the reasons, but talking takes energy —energy that could be used to *build your business*. Perhaps some of that energy that is currently going into words could be better used if you were more conscious of when to speak up. Remember the secrets of focus and discipline. Many entrepreneurs have what I call "verbal diarrhea." They are on autopilot when it comes to dialogue and so their words lose power because "it's just Mary rambling on again," or "Bob's just spouting off"!

Does that describe you?

Other entrepreneurs are painfully shy and don't speak up. They will feel intimidated, nervous, overwhelmed or a host of other emotions. Next time you don't speak up when, in your gut, you know you should have, examine what caused you to feel that way.

As a JW child, I had to speak up at every holiday season. I had to explain why I wouldn't participate in the activities. I had to explain to my doctor why I wouldn't take a blood transfusion. I had to speak up to my schoolmates and tell them why I couldn't go to their birthday party or tell my teachers why I wasn't permitted to participate in a school election.

As an entrepreneur, you have a message. It needs to be clear and bold and ring true for you. You need to feel it in the pit of your stomach and let it resonate with a clarity and power that causes other people to stop and take notice. A little whisper of "listen to me...please..." is not going to cut it in today's noisy world. Speak up for who you are, what you do and what you stand for. If you don't know those things, start there. Then speaking up will become a natural way of life for you and you will also find that a few words will speak volumes.

Question to Ponder:
Do you speak up or keep
quiet when appropriate
in your business?

Success Secret #27

Have Community

Many cultures have a very strong sense of community. Here in North America, we have pockets of community built around ethnic identities. Polish, Spanish, Ukrainian and Korean émigrés, for example, have their community centers and local events, as well as newspapers in their language. However, for those of us who don't have a strong tie to an ethnic community, we can feel lost. Going to church on Sunday is an almost forgotten ritual, we don't know our neighbor's names, and we get caught up in the busyness of our own life and business. So why do you want to have community in your business?

People need and really enjoy a feeling of belonging to something. It's why there are associations, networking groups and organizations. People enjoy the support, the acknowledgement and the framework of community. We are genetically programmed to be part of community and will feel "lost" emotionally without a place to hang our hat in community.

An unhealthy community environment can keep you in a place of stagnation in your business, so you need to look carefully wherever it is that you choose to hang out.

Having such a strong religious community around me for decades made life simpler in many ways. I knew that no matter where I chose to live, I could walk into a Kingdom Hall and have an instant "family" of brothers and sisters around me, which freed me up completely to explore and move and do things that I might not otherwise have done. When I was just 17 years old, I graduated from high school five months early through a special arrangement I made with the principle, and moved from Vancouver, Canada to Montreal,

Quebec, over 3,000 miles away. I wanted to use my French language skills in a part of the country where there was a greater need for preachers. How could I do that at such a tender age—and why would my parents let me go without any objections? Because they (and I) knew that I would be nurtured and fostered in the congregation where I was going. And sure enough, I was.

Although I moved into my own little suite by myself and had to support myself with a part-time job, I never felt at a loss. I was invited out by my new friends, had regular meetings to attend each week, and got busy in the door-to-door work from day one. Any time my family thought of moving or my husband and I decided to move, the first consideration was the congregation. A home was a home, an apartment an apartment, but the congregation—well that was the starting point. Community was that important.

Entrepreneurs today can feel very isolated as they work from home offices, cut off from the normal, typical community feel of a corporate environment. There is no water cooler chat, no lunch room gossip, no catching up in the ladies' room. Consequently, they reach out in all different ways, through on-line forums, chat rooms, emails that never seem to stop, and networking. You really do want to have community in your life. Just decide beforehand what need you want filled through the community and how you can contribute to it. And don't forget to check it out first. First impressions may not be entirely accurate.

"We are genetically programmed to be part of community and will feel "lost" emotionally without a place to hang our hat in community."

<table>
<tr>
<td>

Success
Secret
#28

</td>
<td>

Be Prepared to Accept the Consequences

</td>
</tr>
</table>

One of the toughest parts of making the decision to leave the JWs, after all those decades, was leaving the community. It's definitely a serious decision to leave behind everything that you know, no matter how uncomfortable staying has become. That's where my husband and I found ourselves in 1999. For the previous two years, we had talked about walking away, weighing the pros and cons until we were almost dizzy.

Then one day, we just looked at each other and said, "Let's do it." We plotted our "escape"—and that's really what it was. We didn't feel like we could walk into the Kingdom Hall and say, "Bye, we're leaving and never coming back." We would have been inundated with questions, swamped with encouragement and strongly warned. And we probably would have ended up being swayed. So how did we do it?

We were living in Richmond, British Columbia at the time. We left the Kingdom Hall on a Sunday in September and said, "see you on Thursday," then never showed up again. We moved with the help of a family member who was not a Witness, loaded up the van and took a late night ferry to Vancouver Island where we had rented a house in a small city called Nanaimo. Late that night, we lay on the floor in our new home and contemplated what we had just done. Nobody knew where we were, not even our parents. For the first time in our lives, we had to call on "outsiders" for help. We hired a friend of the woman who had showed us the rental to help unload the heavy furniture. We were totally alone in the world—at least that's how we felt. For a full year, our parents didn't even have our phone number or address, as we didn't trust them not to give it to a local Witness who would come and set us straight! We regularly phoned and updated them on how we were doing, but we were basically cut off from all of our friends and the family.

Nine months later, my husband of over 18 years chose to end our marriage.

I had paid a heavy price for the decision to leave, losing all of my friends, family, and now my husband had just stripped me of the only support system I had left. All this was on top of losing the structure of an organized religion with its strong belief system.

In your business, you will have to accept the consequences for decisions that you make. A decision to grow your business will have a price to pay. The decision to close it down, to take on a business partner, to move it out of the house and into an office, or the decision to expand your line will all have consequences. Be prepared to accept the consequences for your decision. In order to do that, you need to be confident in your decision-making process.

I did not take the decision to leave the Witnesses lightly. In my years as a JW, I had shunned enough people, including my sister who had left 10 years earlier, my father who left for a period of about 4 years, and my sister-in-law for more than 15 years. I knew that I would be shunned and not welcome unless I was willing to come back sorry, take the discipline and follow the rules again. I knew that once we left, what had held my husband and me together—a marriage oath until death—no longer held the weight that it did while we were both Jehovah's Witnesses. Whether or not we would survive as a married couple was a gamble as we entered into a whole new world of freedom and choice—a world we had never known.

You'll be gambling as you make decisions in your businesses. You can size up the opportunity and weigh the consequences—but once you make that decision, be prepared to pay the price.

In case you're wondering: In hindsight, I'd do it again in a heartbeat, despite the high price I paid for my freedom. It's been more than worth it!

Start Small

L ooking at worldwide organizations today like Jehovah's Witnesses, IBM, Microsoft, Dell or Procter & Gamble, you may feel like it's all so overwhelming—how can whatever you do be significant? Perhaps you haven't even started your business or are still a one-person show. Don't despair—start small.

Most networking organizations today started with the vision of one person who got people together for lunch or a meeting. Those people started to invite other people and, before long, there were two meetings at different times and different locations. With concerted and persistent effort, you begin to have steady growth.

According to their 2006 annual report, there are now almost 100,000 congregations of Jehovah's Witnesses around the world. Many of those congregations started out with one person or one family, then grew through their efforts in preaching and spreading the word.

When we arrived as missionaries in a small village nestled at the foot of Mount Chimborazo in Ecuador, there was a small congregation struggling to build their first Kingdom Hall. They were an offshoot of a larger congregation in the neighboring city of Riobamba. Through the concerted efforts of that congregation in Riobamba, they had built up a nucleus of followers in the village. When we left the village two years later, the Kingdom Hall was built and there was a strong congregation that was thriving. But it started with one interested person in that village many years earlier.

Many times, as I work with entrepreneurs, I realize they don't start at ground zero. Oftentimes they are so far ahead of themselves, they are totally overwhelmed, frazzled and stuck—before they've even begun! Yikes! Start small. Get started. Rome wasn't built in a day, and neither will your business be. With good planning, a strong vision, and a fabulous team around you, you can work miracles and go places faster than if you don't have any of those things. But you need to start small and get the engine going.

"Start small. Get started. Rome wasn't built in a day, and neither will your business be."

| Success Secret #30 | Be Hospitable |

One of the Sacred Gifts that I talk about in a CD in my Spiritual Entrepreneur series is the gift of hospitality. This gift is one of my favorites because hospitality is what inspires me to have people over regularly for a bowl of homemade soup. However, while hospitality is one of my gifts, it is also a gift that was cultivated by the JWs. How so?

Each week as I arrived at the Kingdom Hall for meetings, I was trained to watch out for newcomers, people whom I had never seen before, and to welcome them. My family was very hospitable and we entertained frequently—the rich, the poor, the single mother and the elderly widow. As it is a Bible command to be hospitable, I am grateful that it was also a natural gift for me.

As I started doing workshops after I left the Witnesses, I saw how this gift was a tremendous asset at my events. Unlike many speakers who are nowhere to be seen until they appear on stage, I was visible right from the moment registration started. I hugged those I knew and welcomed those who had never been to my events. I introduced the newcomers to the regulars and made people feel at home. It wasn't my literal home, but it felt wonderful offering hospitality to everyone who showed up at my workshop. People still talk about my workshops with fondness and appreciation for the energy that I displayed at those events.

A hug, a warm welcome, and a friendly environment are all signs of hospitality. I've seen apples out on the table at a car dealership, and that's a great start—but having up-to-date magazines on the coffee table, a free phone nearby, clean restrooms, water and coffee available that looks drinkable, and a friendly receptionist, are all signs of hospitality. Just answering the phone with a positive lilt to your voice is a sign of hospitality that is much appreciated and will go a long way to developing your business.

Question to Ponder:

How can you incorporate

hospitality into your business?

Success Secret #31	Enjoy People

Some people just aren't "people people," as my mother used to say. They are far more comfortable dealing with animals or a machine. Most successful businesses, however, are going to require you to be a people person. In many cases, enjoying people is an inborn gift; in other cases, it needs to be a cultivated talent.

Why is it necessary to enjoy people? Animal reactions can offer some insight. Have you ever seen a dog's reaction when a person is afraid of it? Notice a cat when it walks in the room and goes straight for the person who just hates cats. Why do animals react to people that don't like them or are afraid of them? They do so because they pick up on the energy of the person. People are no different. They know when they are liked and when they are not.

As owner of a business or a solopreneur, your people skills are critical. If you own the business, you will have to deal with suppliers, customers, employees and possibly business partners. If you are a solopreneur, it is even more critical because you can't hide behind a general manager, a customer service rep, or a great receptionist. You are everything in that business, and your ability to be liked (or not) is huge. Tim Sanders calls it The Likeability Factor, and it is critical.

Do you like people? Do you enjoy people? Here's an even tougher question: Do people like you?

There is a part of me that is a hermit. I love to be alone and quiet and read or study. I call it my "recharge time," an opportunity to gather steam for my more public professional life. But being in a strong faith community where all different cultures, backgrounds, and languages came together in a family environment taught me to really enjoy people.

We regularly opened our home to traveling ministers, missionaries and families. I learned to strike a balance by having times of solitude for myself so I could truly enjoy people in those times of community. That balance is critical. You will be far more successful in your business if people feel appreciated, honored, valued, and respected—and know that you quite simply like them.

Ask yourself this question: *Do I enjoy people?* Answer honestly. If you don't, and your business isn't as successful as you'd like it to be, then you may have discovered one of the biggest reasons.

"You will be far more successful in your business if people feel appreciated, honored, valued, and respected—and know that you quite simply like them."

Have Conviction

Conviction means that you have a strong belief in something. People today often lack conviction because they are too over-whelmed, frazzled, tired and spent to have much conviction about anything. It takes too much energy to get fired up about much. As a result, apathy has become commonplace. Those with conviction, a strong belief in something and the courage to express it, are often labeled as opinionated. If you're a woman with a strong belief, you are considered a bitch.

We have developed into a weak-spined society. As a result, we allow governments to manipulate us, large corporations to cheat us out of our retirement pensions and religion to control us. We roll over with our paws up like a new puppy when faced by an adult dog because we are programmed for fear and submission. If you are not strongly convinced about anything, you are lacking conviction. It's that plain and simple.

Conviction doesn't have to mean standing on the streetcorner shouting anti-government slogans or streaking naked through Congress—but what do you stand for? If you are lacking conviction, you will waffle frequently on issues and have a very unstable foundation on which to build your business. No one can ever be sure how such a person will react; it changes with the wind. It's hard to build trust where there is no conviction.

Probably one of the most controversial issues JWs are known for is their stand against taking blood transfusions. For decades I carried a legal document that stated that I would not accept a blood transfusion but would rather die than violate my conscience. It took conviction to sign that card and carry it with me at all times. I never left home without it. I had to be prepared to die for my conviction—and I was. That stand was such an integral part of my belief system that fully two years passed after I left the Witnesses before I could finally destroy that card. Although I don't feel that way now, it taught me about having a belief system I was willing to die for. I learned conviction every day of my life. Today, some people might consider me highly opinionated. That's all right with me. At least people know who I am and what I stand for! That's more than I can say for the vast majority of people I meet.

There is a saying that if you stand for nothing, you'll fall for anything. What do you stand for? What would you walk over broken glass or die for? If you don't know, how will anyone else know who wants to do business with you?

"If you stand for nothing, you'll fall for anything."

Be Fearless

Fear is the predominant feeling on this planet. It translates into shame, guilt, anger and even loneliness. People operate from a place of fear on a daily level without even realizing it.

The dictionary defines "fearless" as "oblivious of dangers or perils or calmly resolute in facing them." In other words, there is awareness you may face danger or perils but you possess a peaceful calm when facing them.

The most successful entrepreneurs that I know are fearless. I did an intensive personal development program six years ago. The whole purpose of the five-day course was to have participants confront their fears. We walked on 1400-degree coals with our bare feet, rappelled off 100-foot cliffs, walked on tightropes between trees, and spent time in a sweat lodge in horrific heat and darkness. If you weren't afraid of burning your feet, you hated heights or suffered with claustrophobia. At some point in the course, everybody met fear face to face. Some met it constantly. Courses like this have become common and are truly amazing. But how do you bring fearlessness into your daily life and business? It's not likely most of you will find yourself firewalking or bungee jumping in your business—unless of course your business is firewalking or bungee jumping!

What happens when your values are challenged in a business deal? What do you do when you know that an employee is stealing from you? How do you react when you find out that your business partner is cheating you out of profits? How do you feel then? Or how does your stomach feel when you take on a major corporation or even the government to protect the environment, society or a particular cause—at the risk of losing everything?

Fearlessness takes on a whole new meaning at those times, doesn't it? You see, it's easy to be fearless when all's well. It's one thing to talk about how easy firewalking is while watching it on television. It's another thing to stand in front of red hot coals that extend 20-30 feet and remember burning your hand on that 350-degree oven as you brushed against the side of it.

Being fearless comes from an inner conviction that doesn't always come overnight with the FedEx delivery. It takes time, patience and a continual development of oneself to arrive at the stage where you will not sacrifice yourself for profit or popular opinion.

I will never forget reading an article in the *Awake* magazine when I was just six years old. It was about the religious persecution of Jehovah's Witnesses in the African country of Malawi. Because they would not buy a political party card, they were horribly tortured and persecuted, oftentimes dying for their stand. It was a very explicit article, detailing some of the gruesome practices the government was using to get the Witnesses to bend. Although it was many decades ago, I recall it vividly. It really was the epitome of being fearless in my young mind.

I have no intention of being hung, drawn or quartered for my ethical standards in business, and I'm sure you don't either—but I am grateful for my own degree of fearlessness.

"Being fearless takes time, patience and a continual development of oneself to arrive at the stage where you will not sacrifice yourself for profit or popular opinion."

Success Secret #34	Read

"More than 40% of working age people in British Columbia, Canada have a hard time with the everyday demands of reading, writing and using numbers. This means they may have trouble finding and keeping jobs. It means they may not be able to get the information they need to protect their health, safety or legal rights. And it means they may be unable to read to their children". (Literacy BC)

The average person today spends from five to six hours a day watching television. Reading is no longer the favorite pastime. Yet hit any local bookstore almost any day of the week, as you will see a number of people reading books. So people are reading. There may be a question of what they are reading, but there is no doubt that people are definitely reading again. Are you?

I was fortunate to be taught how to speed read when I was about 12, but my thirst for learning through reading had been developed much earlier. Jehovah's Witnesses are an organization of readers. You have to be. They have literacy classes for those who can't read well and they expect you to read, and read a lot. Daily Bible reading along with a booklet of scriptural considerations, mandatory weekly reading of 32-page magazines, and new books released each year, are just the basics of a reading program encouraged by the JWs.

To succeed in business, reading is important. There are new business books, great personal development books and books about outstanding entrepreneurs that will help you to grow your business. There is a wealth of information out there in books. You can learn a lot and avoid a ton of mistakes if you are willing to read. "When *all else* fails, read the directions," is not the wise course for an entrepreneur.

Reading is an important part of life, so decide today to increase the time you spend reading.

Devil With A Briefcase

Success Secret #35

Study

One of the most common statements from successful entrepreneurs I have read is that they don't just read, they also *study*. Every one of them from Randy Gage to Donald Trump to Robert Kiyosaki has studied entrepreneurs who have been successful. I rarely read a book without a yellow highlighter by my side. Highlighting and marking up the text is one of the best ways for me to remember those passages and ideas that are of greatest value to me. And as I go back through a book in the course of writing or researching, I review the highlighted sections first. That one little hint can save you time, which in turn saves you money.

Jehovah's Witnesses attend five hour-long meetings every week. Two of those are serious study sessions. One hour a week they gather in small groups, often in people's homes, to study a book. The schedule for the material to be covered is the same around the world, and the conductor is expected to cover that material. Having pre-studied, the Witnesses come prepared to comment and participate. The second study session is the weekly study of an article in their *Watchtower* magazine. That session includes a larger group where everyone from young children of two and three, to older people, or those learning a language, can participate at their own level.

It is a tightly-structured study session. A paragraph is read, then a given question asked and answered. The first commenter will answer the question succinctly, then further comments will expand upon that first person's comment. Those further comments are usually the result of someone's studying. Looking back, I can see that it was those who were truly serious about their spiritual development who took the time to do the research and bring the "meat" of the subject to the table for others to enjoy. Newer or younger JWs often gave the first comment because that was appropriate to their level of knowledge.

If you want to be the "expert" in your field, you need to display your knowledge and grasp of the subject. That knowledge comes through studying. Many entrepreneurs today are living a passion or desire without formal training, so fewer and fewer have degrees in their field—but whether or not it is formalized, self-directed studying is indispensable for those serious about their business.

"The knowledge you will gain through studying is the knowledge that will make you the 'expert' in your field."

Prepare Well

A re you one of those entrepreneurs who just "wing it"? Do you "fly by the seat of your pants" in business? Lots of entrepreneurs do. They show up at a networking event and never think about what is going to come out of their mouth until it comes out. They phone a company looking for business and have never been on that company's website to learn one thing about them. They show up to do a presentation and don't have all of their materials ready.

Preparation creates a sense of well-being inside of you. Can you remember a time when you were really well prepared? The files were in order, your briefcase was ready, your clothes laid out, cleaned and ironed, shoes polished, contract run off and directions to the office clearly defined. How did you feel walking into the sales presentation?

Now recall an occasion when you left getting the printing done until the last minute and your printer jammed, you didn't put the car keys back on the hook by the front door so you couldn't find them, the pants you were going to wear had the hem coming down, and you couldn't find that tiny slip of paper with the address. Was your stomach churning? Did you feel sick? Were you all hot and sweaty so you couldn't take your jacket off because the perspiration stains would show through your shirt?

Oh, and because you were running late and weren't sure where the office was, perhaps you lied about a fictitious traffic jam and had to feel bad about that to boot!

Honestly, I've had days when the second scenario is not far off from my reality. But the question is this: Is lack of preparation the exception for you—or the norm?

I learned that the reason you prepare is because you care. You care about the people you are going to talk to, you care about the impression you make, and you care about whether or not you get invited back. When you have it drilled into you morning, noon and night that people's lives are at stake, you take it seriously—and believe me, that dictates a high priority placed on preparation.

So if you are a "let's wing it" kind of guy or gal, or a "fly by the seat of your pants" type of entrepreneur, you may be most uncomfortable right now as I accurately describe your life and business. However, the motto is: If you care, you prepare.

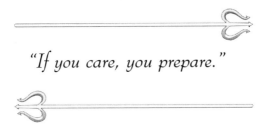

"If you care, you prepare."

Success Secret #37 — Know Your Competition

A re you the proverbial ostrich? Do you want to know who your competition is, learn about them and find out what they are doing—or does it make you feel nervous, even a bit queasy to see someone else with a similar idea to yours?

You can learn a lot by knowing about your competition. Having competition is not all bad, you know, although you may be accustomed to thinking it is. As a matter of fact, without competition, mediocrity and complacency would likely be far more of a problem than it is. Globalization has brought a competitive edge to the marketplace that is driving the quality of service and product brilliance to whole new levels.

Knowing your competition allows you to see what others are doing. As brilliant as you may be, you probably won't think of everything you can possibly do in your line of work. So checking out the competition may give you some great ideas that you can make your own. You can see their strengths and their weaknesses and position yourself accordingly. If you are extraordinary in your customer service and hear complaints about the competition in that area— focus on your strength and let people know what fabulous service you give. If your website is really easy to navigate and some competing sites are like mazes, let people know about that strong point.

JWs regularly look at the doctrines and viewpoints of other religions. They even published a book called *Mankind's Search for God* that was like a mini-encyclopedia on all the different religions. Through studying it, I learned about Taoism, Buddhism, Hinduism, Judaism, etc. Why was this important? Going from door-to-door opens up just about any possibility of meeting someone of a different faith. A conversation will be cut pretty short if a Jehovah's Witness didn't know that a Muslim doesn't believe in Jesus or that an atheist doesn't believe in God. By understanding the competition, it allows them to develop conversations and build relationships.

Knowing the competition in your business will help you to foresee trends, get great ideas, possibly even enable joint business ventures or allow you to send business to each other if you can't handle the volume and build momentum overall in your industry. You will see a motel do this if they are full. Many will call over to a neighboring motel and send you to their competition when they can't service you.

I've recently seen Professional Organizers in my home province of British Columbia form an association to support each other in a new and growing industry. That's working with your competition to your advantage—and to everyone's advantage.

"Knowing the competition in your business will help you to foresee trends, get great ideas, and possibly even enable joint business ventures."

Talk to Everyone

When I am teaching a workshop on selling or marketing, I often talk about a blue-haired pole dancer in Fortrel pants! My pole dancing business was less than a month old and I was at a women's trade show when an older woman, with that blue tinge in her graying hair and wearing Fortrel pants, came up to my booth. The gals in my team standing behind her were having a fit; surely I wasn't going to talk to this woman about pole dancing! Well I did. As it turns out, she was delighted to know about this latest craze as she had just finished belly dancing lessons and was looking for the next novelty! They couldn't believe it. Even I had to admit that it was pretty funny!

I was taught to talk to everyone. The three-foot rule taught in network marketing ("actively engage everyone who comes within three feet of you") was the rule I grew up with. When you are told your life and the lives of everyone around you are at stake, you take your assignment very seriously. Waiting in line at the grocery store, riding the bus, lunch hours at work, waiting at the doctor's office or taking a cab to the airport...I was trained to talk to people about my beliefs. It's why Jehovah's Witnesses are often highly successful at network marketing. Talking to strangers comes naturally to them!

We make judgments about people all the time. We stereotype them and predetermine whether or not they will be interested in what we have to say. I have found that the people I think will be interested or support me often aren't and don't—while those that I think won't, do.

So what do you know? I would never have dreamed that I would have done pole dancing parties for women in their 70s and 80s—that's right, my oldest pole dancer was 82! I would never have believed that the former principal of one of the most prestigious private schools in the city would be among my coaching clients. I would never have thought a 17-year-old aspiring artist would be my youngest client.

What do I know – and what do you know? Stop pre-judging! Talk to everyone about your work, what you do, what they do, who they are—and watch doors open up, left, right and center. You will be amazed at what can happen for you – I promise! Don't forget—I've had old ladies pole dance!

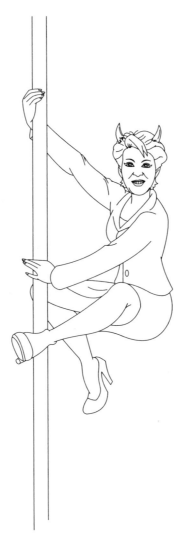

Success Secret #39

Handle Rejection

Many entrepreneurs just can't bear to hear the word "no". Someone says: "I don't want to buy your product; I don't need your service; I have chosen someone else," and we can feel like we are beyond hopeless, totally worthless and a big fat LOSER with a capital L. Does that sound like you?

Face it, most entrepreneurs, even the most seasoned of us, don't like rejection. It hurts and nobody likes to be hurt. I don't care that network marketing companies tell you that you need to hear nine no's before you hear one yes. It doesn't make hearing all of those no's any easier, in my opinion. **No** is **no**, whether it is the first no of the day, the tenth no, or the hundredth no.

However, rejection is an integral part of success. If you don't handle the rejection, you probably won't ever see the success. I know I was surprised when I heard about the number of publishers who turned down Mark Victor Hanson and Jack Canfield's *Chicken Soup for the Soul* book. Are you one of those people that just assumed the first publisher read Mark and Jack's manuscript and bought it? Looking at their unprecedented success with what has now become an entire series of books, translated into multitudes of languages and millions of copies, it would be easy to think it had come easy to them, wouldn't it? Does it make you feel any better about your own last round of rejection to know 144 publishers turned them down? Would you feel more optimistic if you knew their agent actually handed the manuscript back to them and said, "nobody wants this"?

Jehovah's Witnesses handle rejection daily. Have a few doors slammed in your face, have every person you meet in a morning of door knocking tell you they are not interested, and have classmates or fellow employees snicker behind your back because of how different you are, and you learn to deal with rejection very quickly. I still remember that as a child I was taught it was the message I bore, not who I was, that was being rejected. If I had been handing out free prizes, lotto tickets or giving away candy, the response would have been very different. So I knew that it wasn't me—it was my message. That helped ease the pain of rejection. I didn't take it personally.

Today as an entrepreneur, I hear the word no just like every other entrepreneur. However, I don't take it personally. Some of the people that have said no to me on one product or service, have purchased another. Some of them have become friends or colleagues. Others have gone their own way and we never crossed paths again. It's o.k. I don't look at it as life and death, or as an accurate evaluation of my own self-worth. It simply is part of doing business.

Another thing to think about is that *you* often say no. Just think about this as you go about your day. Did you say no to the dress you tried on at the clothing boutique? Did you say no to the more expensive cut of meat at the butcher? Did you say no to the side order of fries at the restaurant? Now think about your true feelings behind those no's. Did you personally hate the salesclerk that helped you with the dress? I doubt it—the dress was just probably the wrong size or fit for you. Did you have a vendetta against the butcher? Hardly—you just wanted a cheaper cut of meat for the stew. Were you angry at the waiter that offered you the fries? "Don't be ridiculous," you're thinking! Of course not. "I'm just watching my waistline".

So why would we think that every time someone says **no** to us, it's a personal rejection? It doesn't make sense when you think about it in those terms.

Rejection is a normal part of life. You reject people all the time. I rejected editors, formatters, illustrators, printers and graphic artists as I selected the team to work with me on this book. I certainly hope that every person I didn't choose, that I said no to, has gone on with their life and bid on further jobs! I would think they realize that my no is merely part of the game of business. It is in no way, shape or form, a reflection of their own value, self-worth or even their talent. I simply had to make a choice and making those choices included saying no to several brilliant, talented people. There's nothing more to the story than that.

Getting a realistic viewpoint on handling rejection is an important part of being a successful entrepreneur. Believing the best in people's motives will also make it easier on you. Rather than conjuring up in your own mind a fabricated story of why they said no and creating an entire soap opera over that two letter word, let it go. Whether or not no is your most favorite word in the world, rejection is not personal. It's part of business, so get over it. You'll feel a whole lot better about yourself and life when you do! And that will make you a more successful entrepreneur.

Question to Ponder:
Do you think that every time
someone says no to you, it's a
personal rejection?

Do you know who was the first female self-made millionaire?

Sarah Breedlove founded the Madam C.J. Walker Manufacturing Company to sell hair care products and cosmetics. By 1917, it was the largest business in the United States owned by an African American. The Guinness World Book of Records cites Walker as the first female American self-made millionaire.

Success Secret #40

Be on Time

Punctuality should be such an integral part of any entrepreneur's life that it shouldn't even need discussion in any business book. But unfortunately, doctors, lawyers, workshop leaders, salespeople, and many entrepreneurs, act as if the only time that is important is their own.

My dad spent some time in the Navy before he became a Jehovah's Witness, so I was raised with the attitude that latecomers shouldn't even bother showing up. Dinner was at 5:30 every night. We left for our evening meetings at 7:00 p.m. and our Sunday morning meeting at 9:30. It was the unspoken rule in our house that you had better be on time. That belief was further reinforced by a very strict regimen of weekly meetings, all of which began on time.

The Witnesses are by no means perfect in this regard, I assure you. I spent four years as a missionary in Ecuador. For the majority of Ecuadorians, time is as irrelevant as the cockroaches climbing up the walls. They get up with the sun and go to bed with the moon. Time is not a priority in many cultures. However, one of the things we strove to teach to the new Witnesses was the importance of being punctual. Why?

Being on time is a sign of respect to your seminar attendees, your teleconference participants, your clients or your patients. It shows you value them because time is money. It shows you are organized and run your business in an orderly manner. And it reduces your own stress considerably. There is something deeply unsettling about running up the stairs at the last minute and arriving out of breath and hot and sweaty because the elevator was too slow, the parking lot was full and there was just one too many red lights!

It's a benchmark for how you run your business, tangible and unmistakable to your clients. Either you are punctual or you aren't. It's not a question that is difficult to figure out.

Being on time is critical for me when deciding whether or not I continue to do business with someone. Everyone is late once in awhile—an accident on the bridge, bad weather, a family emergency —but if it happens more than once or twice, being late is simply a bad habit, and I choose not to do business with that person.

Success Secret #41	Qualify Your Clients

S ome businesses have the attitude that if you can fog a mirror, pull out a credit card and sign your name, you are a prospective client. In other words, there are absolutely no qualifications to become a client in many businesses today. I disagree. Michael Port of *Book Yourself Solid* calls it the "Red Velvet Rope" policy. Not everyone qualifies to be your client. Not everyone qualifies to become a Jehovah's Witness.

That's right. You can attend the meetings of Jehovah's Witnesses free of charge with no commitment. However, you will be limited in your participation of their training program, and you can't get baptized as one of Jehovah's Witnesses until you qualify.

That qualification process includes a thorough study of a primary textbook of the JWs that covers all the fundamental beliefs of the religion. You will do this over a minimum six-month period, usually longer, with a qualified man or woman in the congregation. They will visit your home once a week to conduct a Bible study with you. You are expected to show up, be prepared, be open to the teaching and start applying the principles in your life. If, for example, you are living with someone that you are not married to, you will either have to get married or separate. If you smoke, you will have to quit smoking. If you are in the armed forces, you will have to leave and find other employment. If you don't make the necessary changes within a reasonable amount of time, you will not qualify to become a baptized Jehovah's Witness.

Sound tough? It is. But it is also why they are so successful—they are people who have usually made sacrifices to be part of the community. They are well-trained and educated in what they believe.

I can tell you that the average 7-year-old Jehovah's Witness child can probably find scriptures in the Bible faster than most 50-year olds in any other religion on the earth.

So do you qualify your clients? What do you want? What qualities are you looking for? What is important to you in the people that you work with? What will you tolerate and what is totally unacceptable? The reason entrepreneurs will accept anyone is because they place a low value on what they do. If you don't see the value of what you bring to the table, why would anyone else? The Witnesses believe that you are on the road to everlasting life in a paradise earth if you follow their beliefs. As they see it, that's a pretty big reward for some minor sacrifices along the way. So what do you expect from your clients? What rewards do they get in working with you?

I use this principle constantly in my personal coaching practice. Consequently, I have magnificent clients that I absolutely adore and they know it. Their respect for my skills, talent, knowledge and support of them is amazing, and I love every one of them. It shows! They stay with me, they pay me well, and I thoroughly enjoy my work.

So qualify your customers – have the red velvet rope policy in your business and literally watch your business grow exponentially. My goodness, if a religion can do it in their organization, you can certainly do it in your business!

Question to Ponder:
Do you see the value of what
you bring to your clients?

Devil With A Briefcase

Success Secret #42

Set Boundaries

Rules would seem to be almost a four-letter word in today's freedom-oriented society. But just as it has been proven that children behave better, perform better at school and are happier kids in life when there are boundaries and rules, the same can be said of people generally.

Many people are attracted to the Jehovah's Witnesses organization because of the safety net provided by clear boundaries, guidelines and rules. People from broken homes, drug addicts, and other so-called failures in life have found peace, contentment and a sanctuary within the confines of an organization that is clear on its boundaries. AA has proven this for decades.

How do you set boundaries in your business? Do you play favorites with certain clients or employees? Does the rule of the day depend on your mood, the company's financial situation, the weather?

A big question is: On whose experience or authority are the rules set? The JWs believe their rules are based on the Bible and their interpretation of it. If I am going to be told what to do and how to do it, I better feel pretty darn comfortable with the expertise of the person setting the boundaries. Do you, as the owner, walk your talk —or are the rules for everyone else but you?

The other issue around boundaries is *fairness*. If your rules are not fair, people will balk and rebel. If you make unreasonable demands of them and make them feel guilty when they can't meet those unreasonable demands, they will balk at all boundaries. So are you fair in your guidelines and rules?

Boundaries create safety. They invoke a feeling of being cared for and cared about. They are an important part of the success of your business life.

"Boundaries, when properly set, invoke a feeling of being cared for and cared about."

Success Secret #43	Do the Research

Many entrepreneurs start off their business with a brilliant idea that hits them in the shower or in the early morning fog of waking up, and they are off and running. Market research? What's that?

If that impetuous type of entrepreneur describes you, then research is something you want to start doing immediately. Entrepreneurs, especially those who operate on-line for much of their business have an aptitude for efficiency but not for effectiveness. It's easy to send out an email to your database and hope for the best. But how effective is the email? How would you know? Through market research and testing.

Your success rate can increase exponentially if you are willing to do some research and testing. I too have had business plans come to me in the middle of the night or in the shower. They can be pretty exciting, and it's easy to want to just run with them.

However, the next step for me is to do the research. I get online and check out the competition. I find out through Overture, a word search service available for free through Yahoo, how many people are looking for key words in my potential business. I then go on to search more extensively through Word Tracker keyword phrases and their competition. I may do a survey and find out people's interest. I check titles, price points and what I am planning to include in a particular package or workshop with people who would be potential candidates to attend.

Research and testing should be an integral part of your business. Even if you think you are doing something well, can you do it better? How do you know if you don't test?

Large conventions are a major feature for Jehovah's Witnesses. They have three large gatherings every year, and every four years they have a mega-convention. Having tens of thousands of people in a meeting place for several days is a feat unto itself, especially as that group will include newborn babies, the elderly, disabled, blind and deaf, as well as potentially more than one language group. Streamlining and systemizing everything, including literature distribution, accounting, attendants, the baptism, and meal preparation, is a result of research and testing.

I remember as a little girl attending a convention that encompassed two massive stadiums, one indoors and one outdoors on the same fairgrounds. The convention went for eight full days, morning, noon and night. Over 100,000 people were in attendance. At that time, they provided hot meals for breakfast, lunch and dinner at a very reasonable cost. Over time, they reduced the length of the conventions, because people's schedules and finances needed to be taken into consideration, and they went to less complex meals, then bagged meals, and then to bring-your-own. Changes are necessary in any business, and if you are not testing, researching and modifying, you will find yourself out of date, wasting money and losing clients.

"Your success rate can increase exponentially if you are willing to do some research and testing."

Success Secret #44   Measure Progress

The cost of customer acquisition, percentage of conversion from prospect to buyer, and length of sales cycle may be integral parts of your business, but in reality, I have found that few entrepreneurs measure their success or progress statistically. Their only determination of success is how much or how little money they have left in the bank at the end of the month!

But if you never calculate what it is costing you to do business, the value of a customer in your business or the breakdown of your costs this year as compared to last, you really don't have any gauge by which to measure anything!

One of the most significant attributes about Jehovah's Witnesses is their fastidiousness around measuring progress. In 2006, they spent over 1.3 billion hours in the preaching work. I can tell you that with such precision, despite the fact that I haven't been a JW for more than seven years. JWs spent 1,333,966,199 hours preaching around the world and conducted 6,286,618 bible studies in 2006, according to their annual report.[1] Precisely 16,675,113 people attended their annual commemoration of Jesus Christ's death. Such precision is possible because each and every JW is required to put in an accounting of time spent preaching each and every month.

For 30 years, I reported monthly how many hours I spent preaching, how many magazines, brochures and books I left with people, how many times I called back on people who were interested in what I had to say, and how many bible studies I conducted. I put a slip into a box at the Kingdom Hall at the end of each month with my name on it and the month. If you didn't put it in, someone called you for that report.

[1] http://www.watchtower.org/e/statistics/worldwide_report.htm

It was taken very, very seriously. I never once failed to submit my monthly report in 30 years!

Each month, every congregation tallies those numbers and reports to the branch office. The branch office tallies all of the congregation's reports they are responsible for under their supervision and sends a full report to New York world headquarters. As their year ends on August 31st, the January 1st Watchtower will have the full report for everyone to see. This is public knowledge as you can see from the website link provided.

What these figures enable them to do is to plan. When you are building an organization of this size, you need to know how many more Kingdom Halls will need to be financed, whether expansion will be needed at a country's branch office, how many magazines will need to be printed each month, and what size facilities they need to plan for their annual conventions. You have people to train, growth to accommodate, and money to spend based on these facts and figures. Without them, they would be totally lost.

Are you measuring your progress? Do you know your costs, your conversion rate, your sales cycle? If not, you're not alone. But if you want to grow a successful business and not be hoping and praying at the end of the month that there is money in the bank, start by finding out where you are today in terms of clients, what they have bought, what they have spent with you and what it is costing you to run your business. It will explain a lot of things to you and help you to plan for expansion and growth with far greater confidence.

Success Secret #45

Build Loyalty Amongst Your Employees

As I wrote the lesson about measuring progress, I had to think and marvel at what the JW organization expects of its volunteers! We are talking about *volunteers*, folks—every single one of them—not paid employees! Yet, they report their time and follow the rules. That they even go from door-to-door and do the work in the first place is incredible enough—but to then keep track of everything they do and faithfully report it each month is simply astounding. How many corporations would like to have employees like that? Most of them, I would think!

So why do JWs do it? There are lots of reasons obviously—this is a multi-faceted question and answer. Yes, there is some attrition (me, for example), but many people stay and do what they do out of a fierce loyalty to an organization that has supported and provided a strong safety net for them. Some people may call it brainwashing, but today more than ever, people need to feel wanted, respected, appreciated, part of something bigger than themselves, and supported. They also appreciate boundaries, believe it or not.

On a recent teleclass I participated in, one of the biggest questions that kept coming up was how to hire and keep good employees in your company. My immediate thought was: There are very few bad employees. There are far more bad employers. The problem of employees stealing from you, being dishonest, out of integrity, lazy, disrespectful and quitting has way more to do with **you as an employer** than it has to do with them as an employee. Wow—that's a new way to look at it, isn't it?

How do you treat your employees? If you treat them well, honor them, provide awesome training for them and believe in them and their potential, they will do wonders for your business. The most successful businesses in the world have a very low turnover rate. The secret is to build loyalty in your employees through respect, honor, appreciation and support.

They say that it takes from $3,000 to $10,000 to hire and train a new employee. Obviously, if you have people stay with you for years, decades, or entire careers, there is a tremendous cost savings to your company PLUS increased efficiency.

"If you treat your employees well, honor them, provide awesome training for them and believe in them and their potential, they will do wonders for your business."

Success Secret #46	Be Grateful

Today, the term, "Gratitude Attitude" has become commonplace. We fling around the terms "gratitude" and "grateful," believing that if we say it enough, perhaps it will actually happen in our life. That's a big fallacy. Gratitude is an attitude, and like any attitude, it needs to be cultivated. It doesn't happen automatically any more than an attitude of positive thinking or prosperity.

Why do you need to be grateful? You don't **need** to be grateful any more than you need to be hospitable or nice. So why do you **want** to be grateful? Gratitude is a vibration at the top of the charts on a scale of your attitudes. Fear, grief, depression, despair and powerlessness are at the bottom of the scale. I wonder why? Don't you feel pretty lousy, unattractive to others and overwhelmed when any one of those attitudes predominates in your life? At the opposite end of the scale are joy, knowledge, empowerment, freedom, love and appreciation. You feel like taking on Mount Everest when you are in one of those dominant attitudes, wouldn't you agree?

All of us at some time in the day, week, month or year find ourselves with thoughts of "nobody loves me, my clients don't appreciate me, I can't keep up with technology, there are too many bills" flooding the gateways of our minds. So what takes you from fear, despair and powerlessness to empowerment, joy and love?

The fastest elevator that I have found to get from "my life sucks" to "wow – I feel unstoppable" – is *gratitude*.

What do you want to be grateful for?

Everything. I am grateful for the hands that can type this book, the eyes that can read the screen, the computer that allows me to make mistakes and correct them without getting out an eraser or having to start again. I learned to type on a manual typewriter, so I am not just grateful for this amazing computer that sits on my beautiful desk, but for copy and paste, bold and italics, delete and save. When I was a missionary, I lived in a developing country where one time I didn't have running water coming out of my taps for seven weeks. Today there isn't a day where I don't thank God for the abundance of water that flows freely out of my taps—clean, safe, drinkable water. Get the point?

What about having a Gratitude Journal? Every night just note five or six things that you are grateful for. At first, it may be that you got out of bed in the morning—hey, thousands didn't today. Then you brushed your teeth—you mean you have teeth to brush—celebrate! You had a shower—what a luxury! It's actually quite amazing how cynical, negative and full of despair we can become despite being surrounded by so much.

When it comes to paying bills, many entrepreneurs look at the invoices with dread and shuddering. Perhaps there isn't the money to pay the bill or it feels like all you do is pay bills. Here's a change in attitude for you: Are you grateful for the blessing that the invoice represents? You did receive something for that bill—either a service or a product that you needed, maybe even enjoyed.

Every bill I pay I consider a "Celebration of my Participation in the Circulation of Money on this Planet." That's a mouthful, I know, but read it out loud a few times. Does it ever feel good! What an honor to participate in the physical movement of money along with the richest, most successful, happiest people on the planet!

I could look back with bitterness at 38 years spent in a religion that was often oppressive and has now separated me from a family that I love and friends that I grew up with. I could resent the education I never pursued because the world was coming to an end "any day now," the children I never had because I thought I would wait until I had perfect children in a paradise earth, or the real estate I never bought because Armageddon was just around the corner.

I have chosen instead to make this book a gratitude journal of all the amazing lessons that I learned in those 38 years, the values instilled in every fiber of my being that serve me today, and the deeply ingrained habits that now benefit my life and business. I could be negative, cynical, and, quite frankly, angry at having lost half my life to a cult.

Why even go there? What benefit would that bring to me or to this world to have all that anger pent up in me or expressed through vicious writings? I've chosen gratitude in every area of my life. The Attitude of Gratitude is powerful. It really is!

"Consider every bill you pay as a Celebration of Your Participation in the Circulation of Money on this Planet!"

Do You Know about Memes?

Rhyming with the word cream, a **meme** is a self-explanatory symbol, word or combination that immediately communicates an entire idea. Some common memes are a white flag meaning surrender, a hitchhiker's thumb, and the Red Cross. One of the hottest new tickets for marketing, a meme takes a reader or viewer just a split second to get the point. Like the white flag on the battlefield, it is simple to communicate and it crosses cultural and linguistic boundaries.

Success Secret #47   Admit When You're Wrong

We can waste a lot of precious energy defending ourselves when deep down we know we're wrong. Nobody likes to be wrong. We'd much rather be right. It's a lot more fun, as I'm sure you'll agree. However, admitting you are wrong when you are will help you grow your business. Seriously!

Let's say that you goof up an order to a client. Somehow, someway, the wrong color got shipped, a piece is missing from the order, or it got shipped to the wrong address, causing a serious delay. What do you do?

I remember recommending someone for a teleclass to my database. Many dialed in to listen to the man, hoping to learn something valuable to grow their business. But some ended up annoyed by his teaching style and his long, drawn-out introduction and felt it was a waste of their time and money. I heard about it, believe me! I had a few people that were definitely unhappy as they had come to expect a higher caliber of presentation from my recommendations.

What did I do? I could have argued with them that it wasn't even me doing the teleclass, and said "What did you expect for free?" or defended the speaker a thousand different ways. Instead, I admitted that I was wrong to have recommended him without a caveat so people were better prepared for a more low-key teaching style. I thought his information was valuable enough that people would overlook his occasional long-windedness. I was wrong—they wanted great material and a great presenter. They felt they deserved both and, honestly, they were right. I was wrong.

I grew up in a religion where "right" and "wrong" were clearly defined. The JWs don't do "gray areas" very well – it's pretty much black or white, so I learned to admit when I was wrong. I don't like it, and you probably don't either. It's not at the top of my "Fun Things to Do" list. However, it does keep you in integrity, it will build your credibility with your clients and, in the end, it will grow your business.

So you goofed up with the order. You phone the client and you say, "We goofed up. I am so sorry, Mrs. Jones. The wrong color got shipped and I am sincerely sorry. We have taken steps to ensure this doesn't happen again. However, to make up for the inconvenience, we have deducted the shipping charge from the invoice and have given you a $50 coupon towards your next purchase"...or something along those lines. You admit your mistake. You don't blame the stupid employee, the shipping company, the weather, the government, or the alignment of the stars—you just say, "I was wrong" or "We made a mistake."

People will be shocked that someone actually says that, and they will usually be more than impressed. It's about turning that negative into a positive. Do whatever it takes to rectify the situation, but start off by admitting when you are wrong. Those few words will take you places in your business.

Question to Ponder:
When was the last time you
admitted you were wrong in a
decision you made?

Success Secret #48 — Believe in a Higher Power

*Z*ig Ziglar, Robert Allan, Mary Kay Ash, Mark Victor Hanson, Oprah Winfrey, Donald Trump, Robert Kiyosaki and Ken Blanchard all admit to a belief in a Higher Power. I know "the Donald" took me a bit by surprise with that one, but in Donald's latest book, *Why We Want You to Be Rich*, written with Robert Kiyosaki, they have devoted a whole chapter to their philosophies about God, religion and money.

Donald actually talks about a picture of a galaxy that he keeps just so he remembers the size of his problems and keeps them in perspective. He also says that it is faith in a Higher Power that keeps him going with confidence and humility at the same time.

What a belief in a Higher Power has done for each of these very, very successful entrepreneurs is give them balance and perspective.

I remember saying to a friend, that when you have a small business, you have small problems and small bills. When you have a big business, you have big problems and big bills. Sometimes it's easy to get overwhelmed with so much to do as an entrepreneur. How do you handle that feeling of being overwhelmed?

I talk about being the COO of your business, as opposed to the CEO, in my Spiritual Entrepreneur CD series, and for many entrepreneurs, it is a great feeling to feel supported by a very powerful Universe. Whatever you call that power, whatever you chose to believe about it—from Mother Teresa to Oprah Winfrey, from Mary Kay cosmetics to the *Chicken Soup for the Soul* series, from Robert Allan's success in real estate to the phenomenal success of an international religious organization run by volunteers, there is one common denominator: belief in a Higher Power.

If you have never considered your spirituality to be linked to your business success, it just might be worth considering!

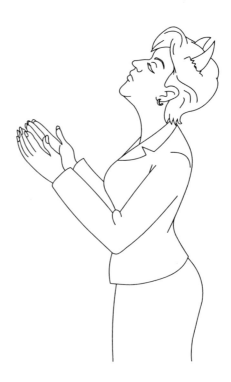

Success Secret #49

Tackle the Tough Stuff

Mark Victor Hansen said, "When you do what's hard, life becomes easy. When you do what's easy, life becomes hard." It's easy to do the easy stuff in your business. It's the tough stuff that many entrepreneurs avoid, often to their detriment.

What kind of tough stuff could that be? Perhaps you need to let go of a client who is taking too much of your time and not paying you a fair compensation. Maybe you need to close down one area of your business. Are you ignoring notices on some outstanding bills that you just don't have the funds to pay? Is there an employee that you need to let go? Do you need to update your look but are avoiding the work of changing all your graphics? Sometimes the everyday stuff of being an entrepreneur is overwhelming enough without having to deal with all those extra things.

Why should you tackle the tough stuff? Because it's often the tough stuff that allows you to grow your business. Letting go of that bothersome client frees up a lot of time and energy, bitterness and resentment that could be used for better things. Suddenly you have two or three clients to replace that one. Your whole business blossoms!

Having the weight of unpaid bills on your shoulders puts pressure on you at a subconscious level. You can feel unworthy to run your business. Clearing up the communication with your creditors will open up the doorway to more abundance in all areas of your business.

A negative employee is like the rotten apple in a barrel—it will cause all the other apples to spoil. Letting go of the employee who isn't working out will help your business to grow and prosper because there will be a shift in energy amongst the other employees.

This creates a more positive working environment at your company.

Because life as a JW was difficult from so many angles, I learned to tackle the tough stuff more readily than many. I don't like it any more than you do! But I have learned when I tackle the tough stuff, when I ask the more difficult questions, when I am willing to face the challenges, life does become easier. And that makes it definitely worthwhile!

"When you do what's
hard, life becomes easy.
When you do what's easy,
life becomes hard."

Become an Expert
In Your Field

A re you an expert in your field? You very well may be and not even realize it! Many entrepreneurs today feel underqualified because they don't have a degree or a plaque on the wall that says they have the "authority" to do what they do. The feeling of not being qualified shows up in the price they charge and the caliber of clients that they attract. So are you an expert in your field? I may very well be asking you the million-dollar question.

What qualifies you to be an expert? If you know your stuff, you can be an expert. In the field of health, for example, you don't have to know every single thing about health to be an expert. Perhaps you are an expert in a particular form of healing such as aromatherapy massage, or in a certain part of the body, such as the heart. An oncologist isn't an expert in gynecology any more than a social studies teacher is an expert in French. Feeling like you need to be an expert in more than a very small niche field can stop you from appreciating the expertise you do have and hinder your income potential.

Why do you want to be an expert? Experts make more money, earn more respect and have a very different marketing approach. Just as a heart specialist earns more money than a family doctor, so too you will earn more money and it will be easier to market yourself if you become an expert in one area and become known for that. You might be the Google Adsense expert, or the Pay Per Click campaign expert or a blogging expert in the Internet world. Perhaps you are a coach specifically for women 40-60 years of age in upper management of large corporations. That specialization is going to separate you from every other coach who has entrepreneurs, male clients and people starting their corporate careers as their clients.

How do you become an expert? When you know enough information about a given subject to be able to speak authoritatively on it and maximize your marketing material to emphasize that, you are an expert.

Becoming an expert is a tremendous advantage when so many people are vying for your clients' attention.

The organization of Jehovah's Witnesses is considered an expert in blood transfusion alternatives. Because of their refusal to take blood transfusions, they investigated and explored all the options very thoroughly. Medical facilities will go to them when they are stuck for an alternative. More than 30 years ago, IBM went to the JWs because they were experts in simultaneous language translation. They had developed a system called MEPS which allowed them to publish their magazines simultaneously in a number of languages—something IBM didn't know how to do yet. IBM learned from the experts at the time—the Jehovah's Witnesses.

Where are you an expert? It may be a very small niche. It could be helping parents deal with a teenage vegetarian in the family. It may be a particular product in your network marketing company for which you become the expert for the entire company. Today it has become almost mandatory that you identify yourself as the expert in a certain field. If you are struggling with this, get some help from outsiders, friends, family, clients, employees, and business associates to identify the area in which you are the expert. Then focus on that field until people know that you are the expert, the one to go to, the best person to talk to about a particular subject. Your business will boom once YOU KNOW that you are the expert!

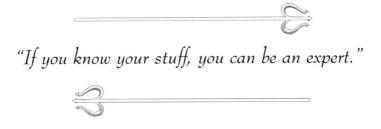

"If you know your stuff, you can be an expert."

Success Secret #51	Take Notes

It has been said that our retention of material drops by at least 80% one week after we hear something if we don't write it down. If you take notes, you remember better. You don't need a dozen studies to confirm that—you already know it! You probably prove it to yourself every day of your life! We've all made the statement "I'll remember that," only to get home or back to the office without even remembering **that** we were supposed to remember, never mind **what** we were supposed to remember

Take notes! It is not unprofessional or a sign of weakness to write things down. Most of the successful entrepreneurs that I know carry around a small spiral notebook where they can jot down brilliant ideas that come in at the most inconvenient times, write down a phone number, a name, a website, a blog address…these are just a few of things you want to take notes on.

If you happen to have a conversation with a JW when they call at your door, they will take notes on the conversation after they leave. They will note all sorts of things about you and the conversation. When they return they will look at their notes in their "Return Visit" book and brush up on the details.

I used notes extensively in a sub-contracting position I took with a major travel agency. I was to cold-call companies in the Toronto, Canada area and try to book an appointment for the travel agency owner with the person responsible for the travel plans in the company. It was a tough slog, needless to say—and as I was 100% on commission, there were a lot of reasons to succeed!

My efforts resulted in a substantial number of the travel agency franchisees that I worked for winning an award for their growth while

I was doing their telemarketing. My secret? I took comprehensive notes on each call. If the manager said that he was going to Hawaii for two weeks, I noted that. If they were using the competition, I noted that. If they were just going to start traveling in their business, I noted that. Then when I called back, I mentioned the vacation, I mentioned an advantage the company I was representing had over the competition they were currently using, or I commented on the potential growth of their business. It was fascinating that many people who booked the appointments told the travel agency owners that they had never succumbed to any telemarketer before until they met me. I had learned as a JW to take good notes and then to incorporate those notes back into my subsequent conversations.

Today in my coaching and consulting business, I take very good notes on my clients so I don't have to ask the same questions or review material. We can move steadily forward. It's a huge bonus. If you think you will remember, you may—and then again, you may not. If you take good notes, there's a much better chance that you will remember.

"It is not unprofessional or a sign of weakness to write things down."

Success Secret #52

Guard Your Mind

If you knew that what went on in your mind was the blueprint for everything that happened in your life, how seriously would you guard what thoughts entered it? Put another way, what you think about, you bring about. Today, people's minds are deluged with garbage through movies, magazines, television and books. The media has filled the airwaves with propaganda, negative programming and fear. Yet people line up to pay big bucks for it, spend hours filling up on it and feed on it daily. Then they wonder why their life sucks! They can't figure out why they are broke or why their business is stagnant.

As much as I can look back in horror at the programming that I was subjected to in 38 years as a Witness and be thoroughly delighted that I have chosen another path, I am truly grateful for the concept of protecting my mind that I was taught from an early age. Mature or adult movies were out of the question for an entertainment choice. My choice of reading material and music were screened. I wasn't allowed to hang out with the kids at school. My television watching was monitored. I was fed a certain way of thinking—morning, noon and night.

Today I live by the motto that you don't get what you *want* in your business, you get who you are. Who you are is determined by what you feed your mind. Garbage in, garbage out. It's pretty simple, but it's not necessarily easy.

The economy is bad, the competition is fierce, it's a dog-eat-dog world—you'll get eaten alive, most businesses fail, you're not smart enough, you don't have the right degrees or you live in the wrong place, are all reasons we are fed daily as to why we should fail. Scarcity thinking is abundant, and abundance thinking is scarce in today's world.

Look at your mind as the most precious of commodities. If you just bought a beautiful new Jaguar car, with leather interior, gorgeous wood paneling, all the bells and whistles—would you haul horse manure in it? No! Then treat your mind the same way. The results of your life start with a thought, and thoughts are fed by one thing and one thing only—what you take in as daily food. If you feed your mind fear and lack, you will inevitably get fear and lack.

I learned to protect my mind from the Devil. My spiritual beliefs today don't include a literal Devil, but I do see the "Devil" as any negative thought that will prevent me from living a magnificent life. I deserve abundance and prosperity, joy, peace and happiness in my business. So do you!

"If you knew that what went on in your mind was the blueprint for everything that happened in your life, how seriously would you guard what thoughts entered it?"

Success Secret #53

Never Think You're Too Young or Too Old to Learn

My youngest client is 17 and my oldest is 71. They are equally amazing in their desire to improve their lives and grow in their knowledge of themselves.

Do you think you are too young or too old to grow your business, start another business, learn new technology or take on a business partner?

When they say "you are only as old as you feel," that's true. I look in the mirror and see the face of an 18-year old looking back at me. I feel better physically than I did at 25 and have more energy than when I was 35. Do you feel old?

If you are just starting out in business, do you feel like you are too young? Are you intimidated by those who have gone before you? Do you feel overwhelmed by how much you still need to learn?

At either end of the scale, there are assets, bonuses, some drawbacks and obstacles. But isn't that true of life? Hello—I'm considered middle-aged, and there are assets, bonuses, some drawbacks and obstacles!

In all the weekly meetings I sat through—over 10,000 hours of formal instruction in my lifetime—one of the greatest joys was seeing young ones begin participating in the meetings. What a delight to watch a little boy, maybe six- or seven-years old, go up on stage and read a passage from the Bible and explain it to an audience of 100 or more. What a thrill to see a three- or four-year old put up his hand, wait for the microphone to come to him, and then give a one- or two-word answer in front of a congregation. Jehovah's Witnesses do not have Sunday school. Children start learning along with the adults from the time they are born. They don't go off and play or draw in a special area—they learn to sit with their parents and to be quiet and participate from day one.

On the other end of the scale, many older people become Jehovah's Witnesses in their 80's and 90's. Some of them learn to read for the first time, go from door-to-door as they are able, and participate as much as they can at that age.

In my private consulting practice, I have a 71-year-old client who knows how to podcast, do a pay-per-click campaign through Yahoo, and has had a web presence for more than seven years. She has just completed her second website with me. She has an incredible attitude towards learning and is more "game" to try things than many 40-year olds I know. Her zest for life is contagious as she travels the world alone and is constantly striving for self-improvement.

If you think you are too old or too young to take your business to the next level, you're not...unless of course you have decided that you are!

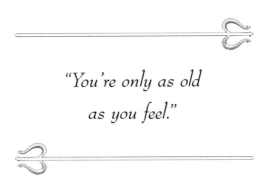

"You're only as old as you feel."

Success Secret #54 — Learn to Eliminate Objections Before They Occur

I'm sure that you can well appreciate that I encountered my fair share of objections while going from door-to-door. *I'm busy, I'm not interested, I have my own religion,* and, *You let your children die,* are just a few examples.

You probably receive objections in your business every day. *"You're too expensive," "You're too small to handle the job," "I don't have time," "You are too far away,"* and *"It's too much responsibility,"* are just a few of them.

In my Spiritual Entrepreneur series, I teach that there are really no such things as objections. I give ways to look at phrases such as *I don't have time* or *you're too expensive* very differently and how to eliminate an objection before it occurs. How?

In going from door-to-door, I would say, "I bet you are a busy person, am I right? Most people are today. That's why my message is designed for really busy people. Everything I was going to say to you has been summed up in this small pamphlet that you can read over a cup of coffee. May I leave it with you?" Objections can be anticipated, even validated, and set aside.

How can you learn to eliminate objections in your business BEFORE they even occur?

Perhaps your marketing headline can be: "Too Busy? Stressed out? No Time? Our 30-minute massage package is designed for the busy entrepreneur, as we come and pamper you in your office. No need to travel, wait in a reception area or even get undressed. Our unique chair massage brings stress relief to you easily, quickly and in the privacy of your own office." Do you see how you have just addressed some of the most common objections before they could be made?

People will have objections in their minds about purchasing product or services from you. That is part of the thinking and reasoning process. By bringing up the objections beforehand, you show empathy. You make it clear that you understand how they are feeling and actually build rapport with them.

I'd have been an idiot if I didn't think that people for the most part disliked me calling at their door. The easiest way to get around it was to simply acknowledge it and include it as part of my introduction. Don't pretend that there aren't objections to doing business with you. Know what your clients are experiencing and address it.

For example, in my coaching business I could say, "Do you feel like you just can't afford a coach? (There's the common objection stated right in the headline.) If you are struggling to grow your business with very little left over at the end of the month, then hiring a coach may be the last thing you believe you can afford. I understand. I've been there too. However, what if hiring a coach made you more money, lessened your stress load and actually increased your productivity? Would that make sense? Maybe, maybe not. I can't know that until we talk about your business specifically. Give me a call and let's see whether coaching would be right for your business."

Eliminating objections before they occur means getting real about what the objections are to start with, then getting creative in how to incorporate them into your message. You can have some fun with this one, so go for it!

Question to ponder:
Can you learn to eliminate objections in
your business BEFORE they even occur?

Success Secret #55   Have Written Guidelines

Written policies, an operating manual, and an employees' handbook are all examples of written guidelines. Without anything in writing, your clients and employees will be potentially lost and your business ethics open to interpretation.

If you have ever played the game where everyone sits in a circle and the first person says a sentence into a person's ears and then it goes around the circle, have you noticed that the final sentence is NOTHING like the original? Why not? Everybody heard it a little bit differently. Good heavens, you can go to a play or movie and hear something totally different from the person sitting next to you.

To lessen the problems caused through misinterpretation, get the guidelines down in writing.

What needs to be written down? Your refund policy, your vision and mission statements, your hiring and firing policies are just a few examples. An operating manual, sales techniques, and employee standards are also required in writing.

Working with an international organization, 306 different languages, almost 100,000 different congregations, and varied cultures, the only thing that keeps the JWs as unified as they are is—you guessed it—the written guidelines. Otherwise you would have the Witnesses in Singapore doing their thing according to their traditions and the Witnesses in England having their meeting at the local pub while the Witnesses in Mexico could choose to have two meetings a week rather than five because of their siesta custom. You'd have anarchy—and despite the tremendous diversity within the organization, anarchy is the farthest thing from what you experience in the Jehovah's Witnesses. A huge key to that success is written guidelines and lots of them. So if you are leaving the running of your business open to interpretation, start writing. Get your guidelines and policies in writing and feel the professionalism, efficiency and unity of your organization increase.

"Without anything in writing, your clients and employees will be potentially lost and your business ethics open to interpretation."

Devil With A Briefcase

Success Secret #56   Community Responsibility

Social responsibility, ethical business practices, and making a difference, have become catchy phrases in business today. All of a sudden it's not enough to make a good living, treat your clients well and pay your employees on time. You are almost expected to have a charitable cause you contribute to, support Casual Fridays, or do some sort of philanthropic marketing in your business. Big corporations and small entrepreneurs, alike, are realizing the importance of being good corporate citizens. It's a good thing and can increase your business and position you well if done properly.

You may be surprised at how many times JWs are the first organization on the scene after a natural disaster. Because of their incredible organization and international scope, coupled with effective communication around the world, they can act quickly. There isn't a lot of bureaucracy to plow through and no politics to play. Since 1994, Jehovah's Witnesses in Europe alone have sent more than 190 tons of food, clothing, medicine, and other relief supplies to the Great Lakes region of eastern Africa. They share with Witnesses and non-Witnesses, alike, as a way of preaching and showing their faith by example. Many times, I remember hearing that after rebuilding a Witness's home after a disaster, they would help rebuild the neighbors also, even though the neighbor was not a Witness.

So how can you take community responsibility seriously and benefit your business while doing something good? Perhaps you can choose one product and have a percentage of sales from that product go to a specified charity. Let your consumers know that if they purchase the ABC line of cosmetics or eat at your restaurant on a Tuesday night (a traditionally slower night), 25% of the proceeds from their purchase will help the local food bank. Build it into your marketing campaign. Get your clients and employees involved. Let them know what you are doing and ask that the charity keep you informed so people are inspired and motivated. Perhaps the charity will allow you to place a small notice or ad in their newsletter or office about the work you do and the contribution you are making to their charity.

I used to hold an annual event in which all the proceeds went to support a local charity. It was a fabulous event and got my company into the forefront very quickly. Today I am working on larger Internet-based philanthropic marketing projects that will enable me to do more internationally while positioning myself as someone who cares.

It's good business these days and it feels good. Double bonus!

Simplify Where Possible

M any entrepreneurs feel like life has become so complicated. Keeping up with technology, marketing, the effects of globalization on your business, and the rules and regulations—not to mention just making a living—can be overwhelming at times.

So the word "simplify" in your business may seem about as foreign a concept as taking your business to Mars.

Simplify is music to my ears. I love the word, I love the concept and I practice it regularly. Looking at my business, people may think it is hardly "simple" because of the number of things I have going—but there is a big difference between the noun "simple" and the verb "simplify" that I think is crucial.

When you think of something that is simple, it may indicate something easy like scrambled eggs, as opposed to a soufflé, which is more complicated. It may even be applied to someone who is very common, humble, or unassuming.

Simplify, on the other hand, is the process of making something less complicated, less complex, or plainer. My business is complex and multifaceted, but my breakdown of it simplifies everything tremendously. Simplifying things comes down to a couple of major questions I ask of every component of my business. What is the RESULT I want? What do I want out of anything and everything that I do? If I'm not clear on what I want from anything I do, I have complicated it. If I take on a project, a new website, a new client, what is the result I want?

The second question I ask myself is: Can I get the result with ease and grace, fun and joy? If the price is too high to get the result that I want in terms of my values, my time, my stress and anxiety levels, then I choose the path of simplifying by either turning the opportunity down or investigating it from another angle. I learned to simplify things as a JW as a result of so many of the training modules and systems set in place.

In a nutshell: Focus simplifies. Systems simplify. Having written guidelines simplify. Being flexible simplifies. If you don't like the feeling of everything being complicated in your life or the feelings of overwhelm that come along, then ask yourself these two questions: **What is the result I want? Can I get the result with ease and grace, fun and joy?**

There is nothing ordinary, common or "plain Jane" about my life or business. It's pure magic. It's an award-winning soufflé, but it has been simplified and continues to be simplified each and every day. I suggest that you write out those two questions and keep them in front of you for a week or so. See if your life doesn't change dramatically as you focus on simplifying your business.

Questions to ponder:
What is the result I want?
Can I get the result with ease
and grace, fun and joy?

| Success Secret #58 | Use the News |

There is news happening daily—are you using it? One of my clients has built a prenuptial agreement website and has written an ebook on prenuptials. Not a week goes by that there isn't something about a famous celebrity not having a prenuptial or debating about whether or not to have one. Can that be used to grow her business? Absolutely! Another client is a financial planner. Personal debt is at an all-time high, personal savings at a record low. Everybody is talking about the precarious situation of the economy. Can that be used to grow *her* business? You bet!

Are you using the news in your business? You definitely want to be!

So how do you use it? Press releases should be used extensively in your business. There are easy-to-use web services that will allow you to send out press releases to media for nothing or at a very low cost. Keeping tabs on what is happening in the world from a headline point of view is very appropriate and highly desirable. You don't have to be a major corporation to do so. Anyone can use the news to grow their business.

If you have a business with a product or service that produces relief from stress (a nutritional supplement, a massage practice, a personal development strategy), then anytime there is something in the news about the increase of disease, higher stress levels, or increase of absenteeism, you have the opportunity to use it in your marketing, in a press release, or in your sales presentations.

JWs listen to the news for one important reason: So they can incorporate the so-called "bad" news into their messages about the end of the world and depict that news as the fulfillment of Bible prophecy. If there is a natural disaster, they will be talking about it the next morning as they go from door-to-door, guaranteed. Why? Because it's a great conversation opener.

If there is a child molester in your area and you are a parent, they know you will most likely be concerned and may be more apt to talk about it with them than if they hit you with a message about Jesus Christ. Your family's safety is important to you, so they use any news around that topic to open up doors to further conversation.

Surely you can do the same in your business! Start looking at the news with a totally different objective—marketing and press releases. Good news, bad news, a small statistic, a major headline—all of these can be used to grow your business. This is a fun and easy way to market yourself and what you do. Are you taking the fullest advantage of it?

Question to ponder:
Are you using the news
to market yourself and
your business?

Have Systems

S ystems are an important part of every business, but it amazes me how few entrepreneurs think about having them or spend any energy creating them. The chaos and subsequent financial ruin that results from a lack of systems is really the basis of Michael Gerber's *E-Myth Revisited: Why Most Small Businesses Don't Work and What to Do About It.* Systems are the foundation of all franchises and the touchstone of all successful organizations.

When Ray Kroc founded McDonalds, he took the epitome of systems and perfected the turn-key system. A turn-key system means that anyone can do it. You can see that when you walk into any McDonalds, anywhere in the world. You have teenagers running the show and doing it fairly well because there are systems in place to do everything. No one decides that it takes four minutes to cook a hamburger if the system says it takes five. Not one employee has to think about how hot to prepare the oil for the French fries. It's all predetermined by the system.

You cannot grow your business without systems in place because eventually you will run out of time and energy and even money if you do it all by yourself every single day. Are you fully utilizing systems in your business?

When someone registers for one of my teleclasses, they are automatically sent an autoresponder. That is part of my shopping cart system. Once set up, I don't have to do it manually. Do you have any idea how much time that saves me? Huge amounts, as often I have well over a hundred people registered for just one class and I don't have to send even one of them an email letting them know the details. It is all done through a system. That is just one example of a system that is very useful, practical and affordable.

What I learned from the JWs' use of systems is that a system allows you to take an uneducated, unskilled person and drop them into a system with fairly good results! Otherwise, they couldn't possibly take a humble person from the countryside in India and train them to go from door-to-door. But they do! They couldn't possibly start a congregation in the Andes Mountains with folks who are farmers and laborers and have them remit that important monthly report. Yet they do!

They teach systems for everything because they have systems for everything and consequently they can grow exponentially. As long as the systems are in place, they can grow at an unprecedented rate. Do you see the importance of systems in your business? It's HUGE!

It is said that at least 80% of businesses fail in the first five years, yet franchises have a 75% success rate. Why? People are the same, the economy is the same and technology is the same. The big difference—SYSTEMS! Which statistic will you choose? If you want to succeed, then start systemizing your business.

"At least 80% of businesses fail in the first five years, yet franchises have a 75% success rate. The biggest difference is that a franchise uses systems!"

Have a Schedule

New entrepreneurs can often find themselves still in their bathrobe at 11:00, teeth not brushed, wondering what the heck happened to most of the morning! If you have come from a very structured corporate environment where your time was regimented and accounted for, it can be even harder to buckle down to a schedule.

You need a schedule. Without some sort of time management, the day will fly by, the week will pass, and even years seem to go somewhere awfully quickly. Do you have a schedule?

What do you need a schedule for? Working—that's a good place to start! What time will you start work? What time will you end? How long will you take for lunch? Yes, this may sound like having a job —but until you create the income in your business that allows you more freedom—being an entrepreneur can be more restraining than a job! You don't get paid for sick time, holidays, or vacation time as an entrepreneur. So a schedule for your work time is critical. However, just as important as the time to work is the time to shut the door to the office and forget about it. You need at least one day off a week—schedule that too!

If you are a one-person show, when will you handle the administration, the marketing, the actual work, the sales, picking up messages, brainstorming and planning for the future? If you don't have a schedule, it won't happen automatically—I promise you that!

At the world headquarters of Jehovah's Witnesses in New York, at branch offices around the world, and at all missionary homes, breakfast is served at 7:00 a.m. on the dot. There is a schedule for everything involved with breakfast. Who is going to open the day with prayer, do the Bible reading, lead a discussion of a daily Bible text, prepare the breakfast, serve the breakfast, and clean up after breakfast. Even the duration of breakfast and who is to buy the food for the breakfast are predetermined. And that's just one meal! **Every single thing** in that entire organization is scheduled—nothing is left to happenstance or whim.

If you look at your business, how scheduled are you? All successful entrepreneurs, corporations and large organizations have a schedule. So if you want to join the ranks of successful entrepreneurs and businesses, perhaps a good place to start is with a schedule—and start with breakfast!

Success Secret #61	Keep it Simple and Streamlined

K.I.S.S. in my business means Keep it Simple and Streamlined. Since leaving the Witnesses, one of the most frequent questions I am asked is one I find most peculiar. It's actually a question that jumpstarted the idea of writing this book in my mind.

The question? People wonder why Kingdom Halls rarely have windows.

At first I was surprised at the question, but then realized that it would seem fairly strange to many people to build a meeting hall with no windows. I can imagine that all sorts of ideas of weird rituals and covert practices happening between those four walls go on in people's minds. It's nothing that secretive. It's pure practicality.

There are hundreds of Kingdom Halls being built every year around the world. As the entire organization is operated on voluntary contributions and volunteer help, they are incredibly careful how they spend their money. Not a bad business practice for all of us! One of the ways they have kept costs down is to simplify and streamline the building of Kingdom Halls. In Canada, for example, you can't just build any type of structure. Yes, it must meet local building codes and regulations, but there are a few models to choose from and a few color schemes to pick from. It's similar to buying a condo before it is built—will you do taupe and beige, navy and cream, or terracotta and brown? Once the choice is made, then all of the materials are shipped as they have been bought in bulk and at huge discount prices.

One way of keeping the cost down is to not have windows in the building. It eliminates the need for window coverings and also windows being broken as a result of vandalism. The Kingdom Halls are very nicely decorated, but they are kept very simple. Unlike a church, there is no altar, statues or religious paraphernalia. It looks like a meeting hall where Weight Watchers, AA or the local Boy Scout leaders could gather. Simple and streamlined are two key words that have facilitated the incredible growth with the least amount of manpower and funding in the organization.

What can you learn from this? Is your business simple and streamlined? Do you reinvent the wheel every time you need to perform a task? I know with the writing of this book, as I anticipate writing many more, I am noting all the steps, finding editors, publishers, printers and assistants who will be with me on future projects. I want to do this process once, have it documented throughout, see what needs to be improved at the end of the process and then repeat it again and again and again without having to start from scratch each time. I've worked with the same graphic artist for four years now. We have a good working relationship and I don't have to explain everything to her from the basics. The same bookkeeper does the books every year so that is simple and streamlined. When you are looking for help or growing your business, plan with the future in mind so you don't have to do those same steps all over again. You can just repeat a successful cycle.

The Witnesses do not go back to the drawing board with each and every breakfast served, they don't reinvent the wheel with each magazine printed or start from scratch with each convention organized. They keep it simple and streamlined and, consequently, are able to grow exponentially with limited funds and volunteer help.

Remember K.I.S.S. and do the same in your business!

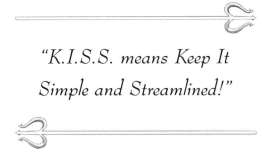

"K.I.S.S. means Keep It Simple and Streamlined!"

Follow the Schedule

There is no point having a schedule if you don't follow it! That may seem like an obvious statement, but how many of you have created a workout/exercise plan, a budget, or a meal plan and never kept it? I bet that every single one of you has! I know I have! It's why New Year's Resolutions are so ineffective. So we can make the schedule with the best of intentions and then forget about it almost as soon as the schedule is typed up!

Why do you need to follow the schedule? Because unless you do, you won't know that it works. A schedule is designed to keep you on track, help you perform better, and save money and time. Those are all important factors in any business, wouldn't you agree? If you don't follow the schedule, you won't know that it has done any of those things. You can't improve what you don't follow.

Why wouldn't you follow the schedule that you took time to create? Bad habits, no motivation, no discipline or little practice are all good reasons why you may not follow the schedule. Decide why you don't follow the schedule in your life and then resolve that problem first. Following the schedule will be a lot easier once that first problem is solved!

One of the most frequent comments I hear from entrepreneurs is that they want freedom. That is the driving force behind many, many entrepreneurs starting their own businesses. They want to be FREE! However, they go about it in the most unusual way. They really do have it half-assed backwards.

In order to be free in your business, you need to get organized, be disciplined, make a schedule, follow the schedule and get your business systemized and streamlined so you no longer have a JOB that you have bought or created yourself, but now have a BUSINESS that other people can run for you!

I follow the schedule for two reasons. One, I get way more done when I do, and two, I can prove to myself that it works. Hence I have a system I can pass on to others so I no longer have a job, but a business.

It helps that I grew up in an organization that took schedule-making to a fine art and following the schedule to an even finer art. Every meeting conducted around the world in almost 100,000 congregations follows a uniform schedule. You could attend a Sunday meeting in Paris, France, in Vancouver, Canada, or in Sydney, Australia, and every single one of them would be studying the VERY SAME *Watchtower* article according to the schedule. It's pretty amazing to see.

If you want to see your business flourish, don't just make the schedule—remember you need to FOLLOW it too!

"If you want to see your business flourish, don't just make the schedule— remember you need to FOLLOW it too!"

Success Secret #63   Have Plans for Expansion

W here will your business be in one year, three years, five years? Have you left it to chance, the will of God, karma, destiny, or fate? Is it too much to even think about as you deal with the day-to-day struggles of business? Many entrepreneurs only think briefly about the future and often do so with great trepidation because they aren't prepared financially to retire or quit working.

Unless you plan on leaving it as a legacy to family, every business should be started with one idea—to sell it. Have you planned an exit strategy in your business? Part of planning to exit or sell is to plan for expansion in the meantime.

One of my clients is a couple with a web design business. When I started coaching them, we determined their values, which included freedom and fun. Consequently, we made some significant changes in their business and looked at how they could create a business that was streamlined, systemized and a business rather than a job. Today they are at the point where they prepare the quotes and deal with the clients, do some of the programming themselves but they also farm out some of the programming work and all of the accounting and bookkeeping. That is just one of the ways they can expand the business with very little stress on themselves. It will give them more freedom timewise and financially, and allows them to focus on the part of the business that is fun for them—actual client relationships.

The walls in my office are full of plans for expansion. I know what I want to accomplish next year in my business. I have three-year and five-year plans for expansion. How would you ever know how to get there if you don't plan? You wouldn't set out on a road trip from Seattle to Miami that had to be accomplished in fourteen days without knowing how far you needed to travel each day. Likewise, if you are aiming for the elusive million-dollar goal of success, then what are your plans for expansion to take you there? How are you going to reach that goal? If you don't have any plans for expansion, you may find yourself halfway through the journey before you realize that you are really far behind.

If you want to stay small, you can still have plans for expansion. Perhaps you want to stay small because you only want to work part-time. Fair enough. What about creating multiple streams of income that happen simultaneously in those same part-time hours or happen 24/7 without you having to work? If you want to become more than a one-man or one-woman enterprise, then you definitely need plans for expansion.

Remember, I talked about measuring progress. I gave you some pretty explicit numbers that the Witnesses have about the activity going on in their organization monthly. Those numbers allow them to plan for expansion.

Plans for expansion have to have a starting point. If you didn't know that you were starting in Seattle, you wouldn't be able to map out the road to Miami. Where is your business today in terms of clients, potential clients, and sales? Where do you want it to be next month, next year, in three years or in five years? Then plan for it like a road trip. Make it fun, make it enjoyable, be realistic but plan for expansion. Otherwise, you don't grow!

"Whether you want to stay small or grow into a major corporation, you need plans for expansion."

Success Secret #64 — Choose Your Friends Carefully

"**B**ad associations spoil useful habits" (1 Corinthians 15:33). That's a Bible scripture that was drilled into my head for 38 years. Consequently, I learned to be very careful about my choice of friends. I have continued to live by a motto that "not everyone is healthy enough to have a front row seat in my life." Pretty powerful statement. But so is the first part of that scripture. It starts off with, "Do not be misled…Bad associations spoil useful habits."

It's easy to think that our choice of friends won't affect our business. One may believe that who they hang out with on a Saturday night does not affect their business on Monday morning. **"How you do anything is how you do everything,"** says T. Harv Eker, one of my earliest mentors, and the Author of N.Y. Times #1 Bestseller, *Secrets of the Millionaire Mind*. Who you associate with as your closest friends will have an impact on your success and your income. Guaranteed! It is said that your income is likely to be the average of the incomes of your five closest friends. That may be a scary thought for many of you. However, it highlights again the necessity to watch your association.

Jehovah's Witnesses have been criticized for their stern approach to association, and I know from personal experience that once I stepped outside the ring, so to speak, I lost every one of my friends overnight. Once I no longer believed what they believed, I was not welcome in their circle. It made my decision to leave tough, needless to say, knowing that immediate outcome of losing every friend I had ever had, but it also shows the seriousness they attach to their association.

"A little leaven ferments the whole lump" is true in bread making and true in your choice of friends. Forgoing the companionship of people who are negative or unsupportive, or are whiners, complainers, or perpetual victims who are NOT good company, is necessary for a successful entrepreneur. So take a close look at your life and decide how important your success is to you.

I admire the JWs' willingness to stick to their beliefs about their association. I have held on to the belief that my friends do affect my success. As a result, I choose my friends very carefully.

Do you?

Success Secret #65

Have a Global Vision

Perhaps your plans for expansion include a global vision. It is so easy today to think globally. The internet has made Sydney, Australia or Capetown, South Africa as easily accessible to someone living in Vancouver as Toronto, Canada, or San Francisco, USA. Have you fully comprehended the impact that can have on your business?

One of the books that most enlightened me about having a global vision is *The World is Flat* by Thomas Friedman. I think it should be mandatory reading for every entrepreneur. It's long—569 pages is not an evening's reading for even the most skilled speed reader—but it is a fabulous book!

I now understand the impact of Bangalore, India on the world. Do you? You should really want to. Do you understand the power behind a company like Dell computers? The author of *The World is Flat* traced the journey of his notebook computer from start to finish. Involved in that chain of events were approximately 400 companies with 30 key players from all over the world. That's a lot of hands working together for just one little notebook computer! Today I have an assistant halfway across North America who performs specific monthly duties for me. I have a researcher in India who finds joint venture and strategic alliance partners for me and does keyword research, and I just hired a project manager from Iowa to put together some of my Spiritual Entrepreneur projects. I am looking at outsourcing every piece of my business to people with strong work ethics who love what they do and do it well at a price that I can't argue with.

That, however, describes a global vision for my business from only one angle.

With proper marketing, this book will be read by a woman in Auckland, New Zealand, a man in Ireland and an entrepreneur in London, England. With some planning, it can be translated into Spanish and now reach entrepreneurs in Mexico, Spain and Peru. This is all part of a marketing plan with a global vision in mind. What about you? Having a global vision is a two-part message. What can you delegate to someone around the world who can do the work you do for one tenth the price that you bill out per hour? How can you market your product or service to someone living in another country or continent or who speaks another language?

As a 12-year-old girl, I traveled to a convention in Fiji and then on to one in Sydney, Australia. As this was a special international convention program taking place in specific cities around the world, they had extra features at the select conventions, including appreciation of the culture of the country. So in both countries, we had evening programs of singing and dancing which I still recall vividly. It really helped me at a young age to have a global perspective and vision in my life.

I spent several weeks in England, when I was just 16, with my best friend, a Jehovah's Witness I had met through a British Witness at a convention in Vancouver some years earlier. The global connection was entrenched in me from an early age as we had visitors from all over the world stay at our home when we were hosting an inter-national convention. Long before the advent of the Internet, I had a global vision because I grew up in a global religious organization that was constantly alive in my mind. Articles appeared in the *Watchtower* or *Awake,* detailing life in Africa or Asia, an animal indigenous to South America, or my spiritual family being persecuted in a country in Europe.

Today that global vision has transferred very successfully to my business. Can you think more globally in some aspect of your business?

Build a Team

A key to success in business is to leverage. What does leverage mean, exactly? It means to make the most of what you've got. Perhaps you have heard the phrase that the sum of its parts are greater than the whole. That's the idea behind leveraging yourself in your business.

One way to do that is to build a team. It could be through hiring sales people so there is more than just one of you selling your product. Perhaps it is through turning over all the marketing to a professional. Maybe you let go of the administrative tasks and bring on a virtual assistant. To grow your business, you can't do it all. Maybe you've noticed that you get burned out pretty darn quickly if you try to go it alone.

Another part of a team may be a Board of Advisors. I use a Board of Advisors for my business. They are people who come together once per month to discuss my business. Why do they do it? Because it is a great way for them to network with other amazing people and the ideas that we come up with to grow my business can often be used to grow theirs or one of their clients. For some, it's a way of giving back; others like to feel part of a team and valued for their input. It's one hour per month, so it's not a huge commitment but it is a powerful part of my ability to grow my business.

You may build a team of affiliates—a virtual sales force that you pay only when they make a sale for you. That's a great way to leverage yourself and build a team effectively and efficiently.

You need a team of resource people. You can use a podcast expert to take your podcast, edit it, add music and post it. A web programmer, a graphic artist, a printer, my recording expert where I do all of my

CDs, my duplication expert and my bookkeeper are all people on my team.

There is a team that leads every congregation of Jehovah's Witnesses. Unlike most churches where there is a minister, priest, rabbi or pastor, Jehovah's Witnesses have a body of elders. In other words, they have a team. That body will be made up of several qualified men who follow the instructions, systems and direction from the organization. It means that no one person is the boss; they work together to grow the congregation and take the responsibility very seriously, although they are all volunteers. Again, it's one of the reasons the Witnesses can duplicate and grow so quickly.

You really do need a team. The solopreneur who thinks that they can do it alone is sadly mistaken. Start building your team and watch your business grow.

Question to Ponder:
How can you start building
your team today?

<table>
<tr>
<td>

Success
Secret
#67

</td>
<td>

Have Faith

</td>
</tr>
</table>

Although commonly associated with religion, faith is not limited to religion. You have faith that you are going to wake up tomorrow morning, don't you? If you didn't, you wouldn't bother having a shower, brushing your teeth, making sure your clothes are ready for the important appointment, or have food in the fridge. You plan on waking up tomorrow, and that takes faith.

The Bible defines faith as being sure of what we hoped for, and certain of what we do not see. In other words, you don't know something for sure because you haven't seen it yet, but you act as though it were true. Wayne Dyer wrote a book called *Believe It and You Will See It*. Most people say, "I'll believe it when I see it." Those people rarely will see it and will always be the Negative Nellies of the world.

Do you have faith in your business? Do you see it growing in your mind's eye? Do you have faith that you will bring in more clients, that you will learn the technology that you need, and that you will earn more this year than last year? Good for you! That's faith, because none of those things have yet happened. Still you act as if they have happened when you have faith.

I have faith that I will sell this book. Otherwise I wouldn't be working on it on a Saturday night. I would be watching a movie, reading a book or out partying. But I have faith that this book will sell and I see it as successful every single day.

Having faith allows you to move ahead in your business. A lack of faith causes stagnation and despair. We can have a crisis in our faith. You may recognize it as the hair-pulling, stressful moments when you lose an important contract, a client cancels on you, or nobody signs up for your workshop. That's when you begin to doubt your ability to run your business, your position as an expert or your effectiveness as a marketer. I call them my Gilligan's Island days, when the idea of swinging on a hammock on some deserted island with nobody to bug me, no worries, no stress and no business seems a highly desirable alternative to the life I lead now.

It's fairly easy for me to have faith in the unseen because I was raised with faith as the fiber of my daily life. I had so much faith that the end of the world was coming that when my dentist told me, at about 8 years of age, I would have false teeth by the time I was 12, I looked at him straight in the eye and said, "Dr. Birk, I will be in paradise by the time I'm 12." We laugh about it every year as I go in for my annual check-up. Dr. Birk retired this year after 39 years of looking after my teeth—which are still the real article, thank you very much! I am in the paradise that I have created in my life, not the one that I had tremendous faith was coming after Armageddon.

People ask me how to cultivate faith – faith in themselves, in their business and in other people. I wish I could tell you that faith is something you buy online at a certain website or in the freezer section of your grocery store, but it doesn't work that way. Faith is a muscle, and just like any muscle, if you don't exercise it, it weakens and eventually atrophies. It is only through constant attention to my belief system, my environment, my thought processes, and my words that I keep my faith strong. I learned growing up to never take my faith for granted. It's why the Witnesses are as diligent as they are in their personal study of the Bible, regular attendance at the meetings, daily prayer, and sharing their faith with others. It's the best way to exercise that muscle of faith.

Are you exercising your muscle of faith in your business? You can't take it for granted as I'm sure you have realized. It's easy to get taken off course, to go from elation to despair with one phone call, and to get caught up in a whirlwind of negativity almost before you know it. It's why faith is so important—even in business.

<table>
<tr>
<td>

Success
Secret
#68

</td>
<td>

Learn How to do Public Speaking

</td>
</tr>
</table>

It's the biggest fear in the world—public speaking. Most people would rather DIE than have to do any public speaking. What's so ridiculous about that is that we speak in public every day! So what is it that happens to our emotions, bodily functions and nerves, the moment we have to do it in front of more than one or two people? People stop breathing, start sweating, say silly things, forget their names and everybody else's, and have their knees start knocking.

The JWs have an amazing public speaking training program. I started in it when I was just eight years old and participated for 30 full years. It's called The Theocratic Ministry School and is very well organized and highly effective.

Once you join, you are assigned a subject and a point you will be working on during the talk to improve your speaking. If you are female, you will be assigned a helper, since women are not allowed to directly address the congregation. (I am NOT going into my opinion on that one!) For example, a subject may be "Why Jehovah's Witnesses don't celebrate Mother's Day." The point to improve may be gestures. You now have five minutes to explain the answer to this question in front of the entire congregation, focusing on the use of gestures throughout your presentation. You are expected to have an introduction, read one to three scriptures from the

Bible, explain them in view of your topic, and have a conclusion.

Once you are off the stage, you will be counseled by a qualified man in front of the congregation on your presentation, particularly on your point to improve upon. You will be commended where appropriate, shown how to do better in some area, and thanked for your efforts. Before the meeting began, you will have handed in your assignment card and your Counsel Slip so it can be updated with either a G for Good, W for Work on it or I for Improved. You are expected to collect it at the end of the meeting and hold on to it for your next assignment between six weeks and four months later.

The Counsel Slip has 53 points of counsel on it. As you work your way through it, your speaking definitely improves. Some of the points are: Repetition for emphasis, theme developed, practical value made clear, effective conclusion, effective use of visual aids, informative to your audience and use of microphone. There is nothing left to chance in their training of proficient public speakers.

Why do they dedicate a whole hour every week JUST to public speaking training? Because they realize the importance of it. If they are going to send their members out into the world to represent them, they definitely need to be trained and be a fabulous representation of the organization. They are also far more effective when they are good at it!

Public speaking is an art. As I have continued to be a public speaker over the last several years since leaving the Witnesses, I have been so grateful for my training as a Jehovah's Witness. I have coached and helped other public speakers and have a CD on effective public speaking in my Spiritual Entrepreneur series. It's an important part of your business. Whether you have to do a presentation in front of your peers at a networking event, do a sales presentation for a potential client, or teach your sales force how to sell more effectively, public speaking is necessary.

Start learning. Get comfortable. Practice the art of public speaking. It will serve you well!

Use Reverse Goal Setting

There are two ways to plan: looking forward from today, or projecting yourself to the future point when your goal has been reached and looking in reverse at the steps leading to that moment.

Forward goal setting doesn't work, have you noticed? You can tell me that you want to be a millionaire in five years and then continue on your merry way in business and in life and five years will come and go and you will be no closer to being a millionaire than you are today. Why not? Because you are using forward goal setting. I grew up with reverse goal setting and didn't even know it until someone coaching me described what I was doing and named it for me. At which point I said, "Oh, I know that!"

Let me explain how I used reverse goal setting as a JW. When I was a pioneer, a full-time minister, I had an annual preaching quota of 1000 hours. 1000 divided by 12 months equals 83.33 hours per month. However, they allowed for a couple of weeks vacation time and so we had a monthly quota of 90 hours. Every month, 90 hours was my goal, so at the end of the following August, my 1000 hours would be completed and I would have some time off.

Because this 1000 hours was voluntary time spent preaching over and above my part-time job, I had to be organized to accomplish this goal. However, because we planned backwards from where we needed to be by August 31st, it became much more attainable than feeling our way forward. Then we got to start from zero on September 1st again!

In your business, let's say you want to double your income and earn $120,000 next year. This year you earned $60,000, or $5,000 per month. How are you going to take your earnings to $120,000?

Divide $120,000 into 12 months and you need to earn $10,000 per month. If you have 10 clients that pay you $500 per month, you will need 20 clients at the same rate, or 10 clients paying $1000. Or you could have 10 clients at $500 each and another stream of income that will give you the additional $5,000 you need. How will you achieve that additional income? If 20 leads per month bring you an additional 5 clients, then you need 40 leads to bring in an additional 10 clients.

It's all in the math!

It's way more fun doing the division and multiplication when you are talking about money, so start playing and figuring it out. Go play with the numbers, then start using reverse goal setting—not forward goal setting. In this case, it's a good thing to be going backwards!

"Use reverse goal setting to ensure that you reach your goals."

<table>
<tr><td>

Success
Secret
#70

</td><td>

Learn from Others

</td></tr>
</table>

Sometimes as entrepreneurs, especially as solopreneurs, we can become very isolated in our business. We get busy, the days and weeks fly by, and we haven't had much contact with the outside world, except perhaps with our clients. It's good to associate with other like-minded people, other entrepreneurs.

In my very busy schedule, I take time each week to learn from others. Why? Because I don't know it all. Surprise! Hate to tell you, but neither do you! There is a wealth of knowledge out there that you can benefit from to help you grow your business. I am on a perpetual quest for more information that I can apply to my business, shifts that I can make in my way of thinking.

So how do I fit it in? Each week, hundreds of emails come into my inbox. I'm sure the same is true of your inbox. Included in those emails are free teleclasses that I can listen to from experts in various fields. Although I know that I will be "sold" something as part of the price for getting the free information, I pick up as much as I can from the initial teleclass and start applying that in my business. I probably listen to two or three teleclasses per month. If you applied nothing but the free stuff out there, your business would grow!

Secondly, I read on average a book a week. I don't watch television, I subscribe to the Spiritual Cinema Circle so that is usually the only DVD that I watch, leaving me plenty of time before bed every night to read for a couple of hours. I take my reading seriously—I usually have a minimum of three books under way at once—sometimes up to seven! Some I never finish because I got what I needed out of them and others I will read in one sitting. I learn from others through reading. A book for $20 can provide you with a wealth of information. Just look at this one!

I also have my mentors. Although they have never met me and don't know me personally, they are indeed my mentors. I watch them, read their newsletters and follow their models closely. Some of my favorite mentors are Randy Gage, a.k.a. "the Millionaire Messiah"; Joyce Meyer, the most successful female minister on the planet; Marianne Williamson, for her powerful stance spiritually combined with a strong voice politically; and John Maxwell for his ability to combine a strong business presence in corporate while being a minister. None of these people have met me personally yet I look at them as mentors.

Growing up as a Jehovah's Witness, I was trained to model the footsteps of Jesus Christ, have the zeal of the apostle Paul, the obedience of Ruth and the faith of Abraham. The whole Bible is really a mentoring tool, so I was raised learning from others.

Learning from others is a real time-saver. Joyce Meyer does close to a hundred-million-dollar ministry a year. Do you think I can learn something from her as a minister myself? Why not model what others are doing well and what resonates with you to your success? One day I intend to meet all of my mentors and let them know what a tremendous impact they have had on my life. In the meantime, the greatest gift I can give them is to apply what they have taught me in my life and become more and more successful.

Start reading, attending teleclasses, and pick your mentors today. You can get books from secondhand stores or libraries, the tele-classes only cost a few dollars in long distance charges, and your mentors are free. There is NOTHING stopping you from learning from others except your decision to just do it. Start today—you'll be amazed how easily and quickly you can get to the next level of your business.

Success Secret #71

Be Accountable

One of the reasons that people hire me as a coach is because they need to be accountable to someone. As much as I appreciate them paying me money each month to tell them what to do in their business, I am still fascinated that accountability is such a big issue in people's lives. I think, "Just be accountable. What's the big deal? Say to yourself that you are going to do something and then do it. Is that so difficult?" Apparently so. But why would telling it to me, a total stranger, be worth more than saying it to yourself?

Being accountable comes down to taking personal responsibility for a decision. Many people obviously find that unless they are now obligated to report to somebody else what action they took, they may not do it.

I learned accountability at a very serious level when I was thirteen years old. That year, I made the decision to get baptized as a Jehovah's Witness. The JWs don't do infant baptism—you need to have knowledge, be putting the principles into effect in your life and be evangelizing, before they allow you to get baptized. I decided to take that step at thirteen. That was a significant decision to make.

The actual baptism is a very happy but solemn occasion. I was completely submersed in water in a pool at a large stadium in front of tens of thousands of people. Over a hundred of us were baptized that day. That outward symbol of going down in water meant that my life was dedicated to God and that I was totally accountable for my decisions. I was no longer under my parent's protective care as a child. I was now an "adult" in the eyes of God, and that carried all of the responsibility and accountability of an adult. I could be punished or removed from the congregation if I did something wrong and I was now a full-fledged "sister" in the community. The accountability of that decision was very strongly ingrained in me before I made it and continually after I took the step of baptism.

Accountability means following through and keeping your word. It also means valuing yourself enough to do what you need to do to grow your business. That is the biggie here.

You've probably heard the scriptural call to love your neighbor as yourself. It's the second of the two most famous commands Jesus offered in place of the Ten Commandments. I've personally decided that one of the reasons we blow up our neighbors, steal from them, cheat them, rape and pillage them, and go to war against them is because we don't LOVE ourselves very much. Consequently, we don't do a very good job loving our neighbor. Maybe we really are loving our neighbor as ourselves and the world is a result of our own inadequate self-love—now that's a very scary thought!

Am I really telling you that your lack of accountability is in direct proportion to how much you love yourself? Yup, I am! Isn't that an interesting way to look at it? You see, if you really love yourself, if you really care about whether or not you succeed, if you really believe that you bring tremendous value to your clients, then accountability becomes a non-issue. You simply decide your course and move forward.

Now you may hire someone to help you decide that course and to brainstorm with you, or you may partner with someone who has knowledge where you don't, but you would never hire a coach for accountability. That part won't be necessary. You'll do it for yourself. Why wouldn't you? You are the most important person in your life. You deserve the best, and the world deserves the best of you.

Success Secret #72	Take Risks

Oprah Winfrey said, "I believe that one of life's greatest risks is never daring to risk." How true! As an entrepreneur, you will need to take risks. It's part of the thrill of being an entrepreneur.

Does your stomach seize up at the mere thought of taking a risk in your business?

You know you should expand your retail outlet, but the thought of renting a bigger space is too scary. Instead, your competitor does it and your business suffers.

You know you should hire a coach to help you grow the business, but you don't want to spend the money every month, so you spin your wheels and waste more time trying to figure it out on your own. You just weren't willing to take a risk and spend the money.

There is a big difference between jumping off a hundred-foot cliff—a risk with zero success rate—and hiring a professional mountain climber, getting yourself geared up with all of the safety lines and *rappelling* down a hundred-foot cliff. Both are risky—let's face it, the line could break, a wind could come up suddenly and knock you against the side of the mountain and so on. But your risks in the second scenario are significantly lower than in the first.

In your business, what risks do you avoid? Be honest. What are you hiding from that you don't want to do but know you *should* be doing? I bet you can name at least one or two!

Going from door-to-door is a risk—you have NO idea who is going to be on the other side of the door or what they are going to say or even do! I have been screamed at, spit on and had hoses turned on me, so it is risky business. Thankfully, in much of the world, freedom of religion is protected by the law—but in many countries, Jehovah's Witnesses risk their lives to attend a meeting or speak to someone about the Bible. It's a risk they are willing to take because *they are motivated by a higher purpose*—a purpose bigger than themselves.

What is your higher purpose in your business? Why are you doing it? Do you know? If not, get that question answered, and your risk-taking will go through the roof!

I am terrified of heights but I have rappelled down a hundred-foot cliff. I didn't have to do it. No one was standing with a gun to my head forcing me to suit up and go over the cliff suspended only by a few ropes. However, I wanted to overcome the fear of heights. It was that simple. That was my higher purpose. It motivated me to take a risk.

In business, there are calculated risks that are necessary for growth. You can minimize the impact of a risk through some smart moves on your part, but you will still need to take the risk. Every successful entrepreneur I know takes risks. They can't imagine doing otherwise.

Devil With A Briefcase

Success Secret #73	Practice

You may have prepared well but if you haven't practiced what you have prepared, you're only half done. One of the lessons I learned as a Jehovah's Witnesses is to practice. As you have probably gathered, going from door-to-door is not easy. So what makes a young child, a foreigner, a shy person or an elderly person capable of doing it? Practice—and lots of it. JWs spend hours every week at their meetings practicing to get ready to talk to you. In their opinion, you are that important! So they learn to overcome various objections and to handle different circumstances until they become proficient.

Do you practice your business? If you are in network marketing, do you practice your phone skills or presentation skills? If you are in sales, have you practiced that conversation with the gatekeeper to get through to the person you want to speak to? If you are doing a sales presentation, have you gone through the equipment you are going to use to ensure you are familiar with it? There is nothing more annoying that wasting people's time while you read the instruction manual to get your projector working!

Why don't more people practice their public speaking? I have discovered that many feel it won't sound natural if they are too polished! Let me tell you, from over thirty years of public speaking training—the ones who have practiced are the ones who sound the most natural. The information is so well-ingrained in them, it has become part of their psyche. It is practice, and lots of it, that makes it sound so natural.

What should you be practicing? Everything! Go through your business and see where you interact with people. If you answer your own phone, practice how you want to sound. Many people sound rushed or low-energy when they answer the phone. Practice how you want to come across to your prospective clients—professional and upbeat. That may not come naturally to you, so you will need to practice.

Do people ask you questions about your business? If so, what questions? Write them down and practice your answers until you know which ones give you the most desirable response. Practice how you give those answers so you sound helpful and informative but not dogmatic or authoritative. If people come into your office for a service, practice what you do with them, what you say to them, how you finish off the service. Will you upsell them or arrange for another appointment?

Practice things like taking their coat, thinking about where you will put it, or what they will do if you are not ready for them. Even escorting them into your office—seriously, you should be practicing all of these things! If you haven't practiced every aspect of your business, chances are good that you will kick yourself after the fact, thinking about all of the opportunities you missed to do better!

Practice can also help you to remember steps in the process you might otherwise have forgotten. Perhaps it's a form that you need and would have forgotten until you were in front of the client looking stupid and unprepared! There are hundreds of tiny details that go into every transaction with a client. If you haven't practiced that transaction, you will miss something.

Jehovah's Witnesses practice because they believe that saving your life is that important. Would you agree that building a lucrative, successful and systemized business is worth a lot to you? If so, then practice is a vital lesson!

Success Secret #74

Live it 24/7

W hat part of the day are you an entrepreneur representing your business and when are you "off duty," so to speak? You may be thinking, "I work Monday to Friday, 9-5. The rest of the time, I'm off duty."

If that was your answer, I would disagree with you. Here's why.

You are who you are twenty-four hours a day, seven days a week. If you are a perfectionist in your business, demanding very high standards of yourself and others, I doubt that you are a slob at home, eat chocolates and watch soap operas all day on your days off and lie, cheat and steal from your friends. Why? Because those qualities in your personality are with you wherever you go. Am I right? You may relax, and I hope you do, but I would be surprised if you were a Dr. Jekyll and Mr. Hyde when it comes to many things in your life. Usually if you are neat and tidy in your business, you are neat and tidy in your home. Likewise, if you are dishonest in your business, you are probably also dishonest in your personal life.

One of easiest things that you can do to take the stress off is to live your values and principles 24/7. Why would that be easier? It is hard on you when you can't remember the lie you told or the story you fabricated. And who knows what face you are putting on for this client as opposed to that client. It's stressful worrying and wondering if you will get caught in your hypocrisy and inauthenticity.

Whether a Jehovah's Witness is renting a movie at a video outlet on a Saturday night, is at the job on Monday morning, or is at the Kingdom Hall on Sunday afternoon, they are admonished to live the Bible principles 24/7. Are they perfect at it? Absolutely not! There are lots of inconsistencies as there will be in your life. Nobody is perfect, not even you! But by living your values and principles 24/7, a couple of really important things will happen in your business.

One is that you will relax just being you. Being in that place of authenticity will translate into a higher vibration, thereby attracting better and better people to you as employees and clients. People can smell a rat, even if you think you are doing a great job covering up your insincerity or hypocrisy.

Secondly, you will have much less stress in your life by consistently living your principles and values. That translates into a healthier body, a freer mind and a more confident presence.

Be who you are—period. Now if you don't like who you are, that's another story. But once you have found and like your authentic self, just be who you are 24/7. Live your principles, your values, and your ethics—and your vision and confidence will increase exponentially. So will your business.

"Live your principles, your values, and your ethics 24/7 and your business will increase exponentially."

Have Ritual

A very successful company I recently heard of has a ritual at their Head Office at 11:00 every morning. The employees get together and have a rah-rah meeting, celebrate their successes and quickly get motivated. It's almost like a huddle. I've seen furniture stores do a cheer every morning before the doors open to the public, and Saturn, the car people, have a ritual of getting together to sing a song to a new owner. It's all ritual, and people love it!

Do you have any ritual in your business—other than having a cup of coffee before you walk into the office?

When I did live workshops for women, we opened up every workshop with Shania Twain singing, "Man! I feel like a Woman!" Her song was the signal the workshop was about to start. I also had a ritual that every speaker coming on stage got a standing ovation *before* they even began. The energy level in the room was raised, the speaker felt fabulous before they even began, and it set a high level of expectation for the workshop. After lunch, we always had a dance time when everybody in the room was bopping and hopping, shaking and moving to some upbeat song. The women attendees got to expect this ritual, and although some felt uncomfortable the first time around, they came to expect and enjoy it.

Can you have a ritual in your business? Perhaps every client gets a personalized birthday card from you. Maybe you give away something for free every Christmas to your client base. You could have a special meeting every Friday afternoon where the top salesperson gets to share their best appointment of the week with the other salespeople and everybody applauds their success. A ritual is only limited by your creativity. Make it fun. Make it meaningful to you and to your clients.

Why are rituals so important? They bring a level of comfort to people because they always happen. So they feel safe and secure—two important things people need to feel in order to buy. Secondly, it builds community, which is really important to keep people loyal to you and your company. Thirdly, people enjoy them!

I've seen people at a workshop shake their heads and roll their eyes the first time they were shown how to clap a certain rhythm or turn to their neighbor and give them a high-five! But I've also seen those same people by day two of a workshop up on stage dancing, giving people high-fives on the way to the restroom and hugging total strangers before they went home. Ritual brings out the best in people. There is something genetically programmed into us to make rituals evoke a deep sense of belonging.

Used for the good, rituals can be highly effective in your business, whether you do something specific at your workshops, create something for your employees, or have a ritual that you do for yourself as a solopreneur.

Growing up in a religion with ritual gave me a sense of community. Opening and closing every meeting with prayer was a ritual. Gathering together as a group before going from door-to-door was a ritual. I felt secure in those rituals.

Think about how you can implement rituals in your business.

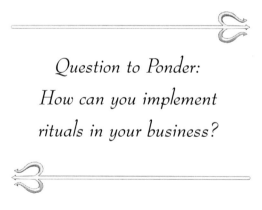

Question to Ponder:
How can you implement
rituals in your business?

Be Well-groomed

I n his book *Sales Dogs*, Blair Singer cites studies indicating that well-groomed and well-dressed salespeople sell up to 35 percent more than those who do not take such pride in their appearance.

Your appearance counts. I am not talking about wearing Prada or Gucci or whatever is the fashion flavor-of-the-month, but I am talking about something very important.

One of the points that was included in my public speaking training was personal appearance. Jehovah's Witnesses are fanatical about their standard of grooming. Unlike many churches where people show up in jeans, casual pants or even shorts, the standard of dress amongst the JWs has been commented on by media around the world.

I attended every single JW meeting for 38 years in a dress or skirt. I never once wore a pair of pants to a Kingdom Hall or convention. Men wear suits to the meetings, complete with neckties. Just as I wouldn't have dreamed of going to a meeting in a pantsuit, a man wouldn't even think of showing up in a casual pair of pants and sports shirt. Why do they take it so seriously? For them, it is a question of respect for a place of worship and the God they believe they represent. Secondly, it is an example. They are very conscious about standing apart from the rest of the world. Remember, they think they are the only true religion, and they take that distinction very seriously. Their physical dress is an obvious way to set themselves apart from the rest.

How do you feel about your appearance? Do you run out to meet a client with your hair not done or without make-up because they have been with you forever and they don't care? My goodness, they're practically friends! One of my clients got caught dressing down for an important meeting because she had seen the employees dressed quite casually. However, when she showed up, all the top executives were in formal business wear. She felt uncomfortable in her smart but casual pants and top. Not what she needed for a boost of confidence as she walked into an important meeting!

If the study is even close to being right—that you can sell as much as 35 percent more than those who don't take care about their grooming—that's a significant chunk of change in your pocket for just caring about what you look like. A 35 percent increase for many entrepreneurs is in the tens of thousands of dollars.

You don't have to wear the top designers and look like you just stepped out of *Vogue* magazine. It may not even be appropriate for your line of business to be in a dress and high heels or a suit. But being well-groomed means presenting yourself well, with up-to-date clothing that is clean and well-pressed, with shoes shined, hair combed and styled, and make-up that is suitable for your age and facial features. I have to color my hair every four weeks or I have gray roots. I have to have it cut every six weeks. If my hair doesn't look good, I don't feel good, and that one grooming faux pas translates into less confidence.

Look in the mirror and be honest. Do you need an updated haircut? Do you need a makeover? Go stand in your closet and decide what goes and what stays. Then buy one or two really nice pieces of clothing that make you feel like a million dollars when you put them on. Think the whole outfit through from your jewelry to your shoes. This has nothing to do with money. There are some amazing secondhand stores that sell beautiful clothing for pennies on the dollar, and sales happen all year round.

If you don't have good taste in clothing, find a friend who does and take him or her shopping with you. Men, if you are colorblind—and there are more of you who are colorblind than there are women— take someone who knows the difference between navy and black shopping with you. Be sure that your socks match your shoes and that both match your pants if it's a business look you're after. If you are an artist selling pottery, having mismatched socks may be totally cool and appropriate. But take your appearance seriously, nonetheless.

Have fun with this while realizing that your grooming is an important part of your business!

"Well-groomed and well-dressed salespeople sell up to 35 percent more than those who do not take such pride in their appearance."

Do you know what a social entrepreneur is?

The job of a **social entrepreneur** is to find what is not working and solve the problem by changing the system, spreading the solution and persuading entire societies to take new leaps. Social entrepreneurs are not content just to give a fish or teach how to fish. They will not rest until they have revolutionized the fishing industry. Florence Nightingale, Margaret Sanger and Muhammad Yunus are all social entrepreneurs. They changed their industry.

Cleanliness

There's a familiar saying that "cleanliness is next to godliness." Cleanliness is relative. Someone reading this book in a developing nation without access to a hot daily shower, living with dirt roads and without deodorant will have a different concept of cleanliness from someone living in a country where clean water flows freely and soap and deodorant are readily available and relatively inexpensive.

But as an entrepreneur out meeting people, cleanliness is not to be taken lightly. Most of us have been guilty of bad breath once in awhile, unpleasant body odor or nails in need of a manicure. If you are tempted to skip this chapter and say, "This doesn't apply to me," please don't. It may not be you personally. It might be one of your salespeople who smokes and then walks into a client's office smelling of smoke. It could be that the office in which you see clients isn't as clean as it could be. It may be that your car has seen better days.

My home is immaculate—my car can be another story. We all have our Achilles heel—so although talking about b.o., bad breath and dirt under your fingernails may not be comfortable for you, you may be losing clients because of it.

There is a woman I know who is fairly successful but reeks of body odor. If I get too close to her at a seminar or event, I literally have to hold my breath. Her clothes smell like they haven't had a dry cleaning in years! Other times, a salesperson has leaned over to show me details on a contract and immersed me in a cloud of really bad breath. I automatically lean back. What about you?

You may be thinking—how would I know if I have a problem? Cup your hands over your mouth and breathe into your hands, then smell. If it's not pleasant, there's a clue. Lift up your arms and smell. If it's not coming up roses, buy a different brand of deodorant. Send your clothes to the dry cleaners or wash more frequently. I also replace my t-shirts, sweaters and anything that is close to my underarms on a regular basis. Just being aware of this as a potential problem is important.

Even men these days have manicures to ensure that their nails look good. Hangnails, bitten nails and dirt under your nails are not acceptable for men or women. Pointing out features on a contract, signing a deal, or working on someone's body as a massage therapist is going to bring your hands into full view. Are you embarrassed by what you see? What kind of impression are your hands making? I know, because I have horrible nails—so I have my nails done on a regular basis. What a relief to stop sitting on my hands, embarrassed by how ugly they looked! My confidence went through the roof when I started to look after my nails.

JWs talk about this kind of stuff regularly. They will have articles in their magazines about personal hygiene or talks at their meetings about the importance of cleanliness. They don't brush it under the carpet, hoping every person in their organization will brush their teeth, use deodorant and bathe daily. Although they understand the difference in cultures, cleanliness in that organization is not optional. It shouldn't be optional in your business either!

Success Secret #78   Take A Stand – Be Resolute

How many of you know that Jehovah's Witnesses don't vote in government elections? It's one of the few things I have yet to participate in since leaving the Witnesses. I still have never voted.

JWs don't vote because they believe they have already voted symbolically—by their actions—for God's government. I know, I know, trust me. I can still shake my head at what I believed, but that's not the point here. The issue is their incredibly resolute stand. Do you know that many Witnesses have been killed, tortured, fired from their jobs or imprisoned because of their resoluteness on certain issues? They will not go to war and they will not vote. Plain and simple and absolutely unquestionable in their eyes.

Where do you need to take a stand in your business? Have you put up with a shoddy supplier because they were cheaper than the next guy? Have you been shirking your responsibilities from an environmental standpoint because it might make you some enemies in your community? It could even be as simple as saying NO to your clients about working on weekends because that is family time.

Think about where you have taken a stand. Are you resolute in your conviction? Do you still feel that strongly about it, or did you just put a policy in place years ago that you haven't gotten around to updating to harmonize with your current beliefs? Are you embarrassed to change a position you have firmly held for years because it's so different, and people might think you are flaky? Yet every time you think about that issue, you cringe at what you have said or written.

These are all questions that every entrepreneur needs to consider. I said and did lots of things over those 38 years that make me smile today, shake my head and recoil in horror at how convinced I was of my "rightness" and everyone else's "wrongness." As I have had to completely lay a new foundation for my life, I have changed my mind many times over the past seven years as I figured out my new position on everything from horoscopes and psychics to sex and marriage to honesty and integrity. I haven't always come up with my final stand right out of the gate, and have had to retract, review and renege on some promises because of asking myself those very same questions.

Taking a stand for better or for worse is important in business. It gives you a barometer for your values and principles, but it also gives people around you something by which to gauge who you really are. That is becoming more and more important today in business.

Question to Ponder:
Where do you need to take
a stand in your business?

Success Secret #79

Get Comfortable with Being Uncomfortable

I am sure I was the only ten-year-old who knew the meaning of words such as circumcision, menstruation, and masturbation, as well as the distinctly technical difference between fornication and adultery. Because the JWs don't separate the children from the adults at their meetings, a talk on sex and marriage is heard by a six-year-old along with the sixty-year-old.

A discussion of the sanctity of blood could easily include a discussion of menstruation, and a talk on the difference between a Jew and a Gentile would likely mention circumcision. Just about everything is discussed between the four walls of any Kingdom Hall!

Fairly soon after leaving the Witnesses, I went on to promote a "female Viagra-type product" through a network marketing company. I have to say that I was stunned at how embarrassed and reticent women were, discussing their anatomy and sexual behavior. Talking about clitorises and orgasms came as naturally to me as discussing having fried chicken and mashed potatoes for dinner. I then realized my upbringing had definitely made me comfortable discussing what is uncomfortable for many people.

Being an entrepreneur will take you out of your comfort zone more times than not. From what I can see after more than 25 years, there is nothing comfortable about being an entrepreneur. You will feel pressured to keep up with technology and have demands placed upon you to know it all and figure it out for yourself. And you will be the only one responsible for bringing in the money. None of that is comfortable for someone who has come from a corporate setting where there is always someone higher up to turn to for guidance, advice and help.

So getting comfortable with the uncomfortable is critical to your growth. You can't stay in the little box forever and grow, anymore than a baby can sleep in a crib for the rest of their life. They have to move out into something bigger! So do you!

What's uncomfortable in your business that is keeping you small? What are you putting off learning because it doesn't suit you? Is there something embarrassing or uncomfortable you have been avoiding that needs to be discussed with an employee or client?

Decide today you are going to get comfortable with the uncomfortable in your life. Deal with what is holding you back and before you know it, you'll be comfortable with what was once uncomfortable.

Question to Ponder:
What area of your business
are you uncomfortable with
that you need to get
comfortable with?

Have Fun

Jehovah's Witnesses don't celebrate any of the holidays. I mean none—not Christmas, not Easter, not Halloween, none of them. Now they have their reasons for not celebrating these holidays, but from most people's viewpoint, it would seem like there was not much fun in the life of a typical JW—just a lot of hard work.

Have you ever asked yourself, "What is fun for me?" Do you know what you really classify as "fun"? Fun is something that you enjoy— something that makes you feel good about yourself, about life or what you are doing.

So do you have fun in your business? I know I do. I love my clients and they thoroughly enjoy having me as their coach. I laugh with my clients, I joke with them, I love what I do and it shows.

Lots of entrepreneurs don't have fun. They take being an entrepreneur very seriously and walk around like they have the weight of the world on their shoulders. They talk seriously, act seriously and always seem to be complaining about how hard business is or how tough it is to get clients. Yikes—I usually can't wait to get away from them as quickly as possible! I'm not surprised that nobody wants to hang out with them.

As I said to one client—"why would anyone want to be with you – you think you are a bitch and so do they!" She burst out laughing and shouted, "You're so right!" "I know," I replied "so let's change that right now. Lighten up! Have fun and stop being so miserable about everything."

I probably have more fun than many entrepreneurs because I have been doing this for a long time—more than a quarter century now

—so I am fairly seasoned at the cycles of business. I also appreciate each day more than the majority, simply because I wasn't supposed to be here at this age or at this time in the calendar. Armageddon was always coming, so I seriously never thought I would be here in late 2006 and finishing my first book. After bearing a rather ominous message every day for 38 years, my life feels like fun before I even get out of bed in the morning!

However, I also learned to have fun as I was growing up just working and being who I was. Every meeting was a very social event. We got to the Kingdom Hall early so we could visit and often stayed visiting for thirty minutes afterwards, even though they were school nights. Getting home at 10:00 p.m. from a meeting was normal. As hospitality was a large part of our life, we often had people coming over for dinner as well as parties or social events to attend. I never got one birthday present from my parents or had one Christmas morning, but they took me traveling all over the world.

On Halloween night, I remember going down to the beach close to where we lived and having a congregation party complete with bonfire and roasted hotdogs and marshmallows. Because we wouldn't open the door to hand out candy, none of us wanted to be home, so it was one way to avoid the trick-or-treaters and get out and have fun in a way that was acceptable.

Having fun was completely a state of mind. Attending an eight-day convention with 100,000 other attendees, helping to serve meals at the convention, seeing friends from all over the city, watching a Bible drama acted out in full costume, and then coming home to a house full of guests from all over the world who were staying with us to attend the convention in my city—those were highlights of my childhood. Going from door-to-door as a young child and getting to ring the doorbell was fun. We'd go for a coffee break and I'd get a hot chocolate and a donut and meet up with my friends who were out working other streets. That was fun. It was a lot of little things that made life fun, even the work.

You bet I was excited at my first birthday party, and I was like a little kid decorating my first Christmas tree. I had a blast learning about the idiosyncrasies of Christmas crackers and learning to sing Christmas carols for the first time. It's all been fun, but that's largely because I see every day as fun. Even work is fun. Work may even be the most fun! That's a state of mind—one I am really glad I had instilled in me right from infancy.

"Having fun in your business is completely a state of mind."

Do you know about these important shifts in marketing?

In 2005, one U.S. rock radio station went out of business each week. Hollywood box office sales fell 7 percent in 2005, newspaper readership fell by 3 percent, magazine newsstand sales are at their lowest level in more than 30 years and even the 2006 Winter Olympics had its lowest ratings in twenty years, down 37 percent from the 2002 Games.

Success Secret #81	Teach Others

Teaching others to do what you do is the greatest gift you can give yourself and others. A person living in fear refuses to teach someone else what they themselves know because the student may surpass the teacher. A good teacher encourages his student to excel, even if that means the student exceeds the teacher. Teaching others is critical if you want to grow your business.

This is a common tool used in network marketing. It is all about duplication, duplication, duplication. If you don't teach others, you have no duplication. In most businesses, you will need to delegate tasks to others. To grow your business, you cannot continue to do it all yourself, even if you try! Delegation requires teaching others.

Some people do not have the gift of teaching. You listen to someone who doesn't have the gift and your eyes glaze over as they drone on. If you don't have the gift of teaching, you may want to write down the information. If you don't have the gift of writing either, then you can convey the information to someone who does have the gift of teaching or writing and put it into a manual.

The important thing is that somewhere in your business you are focused on teaching others.

Teaching others is probably one of the biggest, most important reasons for the success of the Jehovah's Witnesses. They are dedicated to the teaching of others. It is their whole purpose for existence. Through their magazines, books, brochures, pamphlets, meetings, and conventions, they are truly a teaching organization. They believe that everyone is capable of learning, and of course they are. Some will do better than others. Each has individual gifts, and the JWs recognize that.

The word "charismatic" actually comes from the Bible word "charism" which means a "divinely conferred gift or power." So a truly gifted teacher will be very charismatic. Perhaps that describes you.

Teaching others what you know empowers others. It removes the stress from you to have to do it all yourself. It positions you as a leader, which is a good thing. Look at your own business and decide where you can teach others. Is it by delegating a task, training your employees better, or improved education of your prospective and existing clients? Every one of those areas will improve your bottom line and happiness quotient while growing your business. And that's what it's all about!

Success Secret #82

Review

It's easy to let one year after another go by without really stopping to take stock of what happened that year. I start reviewing my year in November and spend a good six weeks reviewing what happened since January and planning for the New Year. Are you reviewing your business consistently? It's easy to get busy "doing it, doing it, doing it," as Michael Gerber of *The E-Myth* fame says. We are so busy being the technician in our business that we forget to be the visionary and planner. It's hard to plan when you have never reviewed.

I like to do a written review. It's probably why journaling is an integral part of my life. I write in my journal almost every single day. That is my written review on a daily basis, and it helps me to analyze the day and review it in my own mind while getting it down on paper. Then at the end of the year, I really review where I have gone, what I have accomplished, what I am the most pleased about and where I want to improve.

At least four times per year while I was growing up, the Jehovah's Witnesses did a written review of what we had learned in our public speaking training. It was called, sensibly enough, *The Written Review*. We received a double-sided form with true-false questions, matching questions, short essays, and fill-in-the-blanks. We completed the exam in thirty minutes, then spent the next twenty minutes going over the answers, participating and discussing any difficult or less-than-obvious answers. Nobody checked on you—this was all self-evaluation—but it was an integral part of my growing up. Had I been paying attention? Was I learning anything? How much did I remember? Those are good questions in every business, don't you think?

One of my clients actually includes in her business plan each year what technology she wants to learn that year. Using my time management system allows me to review each week and know if I am moving toward my goals, as my objectives for the week are clearly identified in my daytimer.

Do a review of your business regularly. Have a look at your Cash Flow Analysis and Profit and Loss Statements and go over your business plan. None of these should be stagnant pieces of paper in your office. They should be dynamic and fresh in your mind. I have my office walls plastered with large sheets (2' x 3') of paper that have my goals, directions, business plans, and current projects outlined for my constant review. It means that even when I am working, my subconscious is already noting what needs to be done next, what's coming up, and where I am headed, so that everything is constantly moving forward.

There's a rule in tailoring that I learned in high school that is guaranteed to save you from a sewing disaster: *Measure twice, cut once.* Reviewing your business will do the same for you as an entrepreneur.

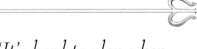

"It's hard to plan when
you have never reviewed."

Use Discernment

You've probably heard someone say, "He is like a bull in a china shop." What does that mean? It means someone is too rambunctious, too outspoken, treading over everything and everyone. It also means that they are not wanted. Are you like a bull in a china shop in some area of your business?

I can tell you right now that there are JWs who act like a bull in a china shop when it comes to honoring your beliefs. I know—I have been with them at the door when they didn't listen to you. They could be highly opinionated, even literally putting their foot in your door so you couldn't close it! I can also tell you that they are the exception, not the rule. JWs really are trained to be discerning, to be aware of taking up your time, the weather conditions as you open the door and your overall attitude.

Discernment means an acuteness of judgment and understanding, the act of exhibiting keen insight. That means seeing beyond what is said, using good judgment and knowing when to say something and when to shut up.

How's your level of discernment?

Suppose you hear an employee say something to a potential client that is not quite accurate. As the owner, do you rush in and say that the employee doesn't know what she's talking about? No, that would not be discerning. If appropriate, you could step in, introduce yourself as the owner and have a chat with the person to clarify the situation. You might even leave it until later, then take the employee aside and offer the accurate information.

The other day I complained to an employee that their store keeps moving a product I buy from them. One day it is in the front of the store; the next time it's in the refrigerator at the back of the store; the time after that it's on the shelf in the middle of the store. It was frustrating to be looking for the same product in the same store for the third time and not finding it.

I mentioned this to the young man who was leading me to the latest place for the item. He replied, "Well that's the crazy management we have at this store." I cringed. Even if it was true, it represented a serious lack of discernment on the part of that employee. You just don't say things like that to a customer. You say, "I appreciate how you feel. I will mention that to management at our next staff meeting. Thank you—and here is what you are looking for, Miss."

I remember training a receptionist who lacked discernment when she said, "Mr. Alexander has just gone to the bathroom." That's not what I want to envision as Mr. Alexander's client. Sorry, but even something as simple as comments like that are important to the image of your business. It would be much more professional to say, "Mr. Alexander has just stepped out of the office for a moment. Can I have him return the call, please?" I have people tell me how little money they make, their personal problems or their health challenges. Even though it may all be true, as a prospective Joint Venture partner, it may not be appropriate, as it does not build my confidence in you or in your business. Discernment is knowing what to say and when to say it. If you have any doubts in this area, ask a friend to give you some feedback. It's an area I am always working on because it's critically important. You really don't want to be known as a bull in a china shop!

"Discernment means seeing beyond what is said, using good judgment and knowing when to say something and when to shut up. "

Success Secret #84

Take the Lead

D o you wait for other people to show up in your business, or do you take the lead? That could mean something as simple as getting into your office before 9:00 every morning when there is no one telling you that you have to. It could also mean being the one to organize an association, start contributing to a charity as part of your marketing program, or volunteering to chair your networking group for the year. Ask yourself: Do I sit around and wait for other people to do things, or do I make them happen?

Are you a leader?

Not everyone is a leader, naturally. But just like any skill that is required to run a business, leadership is one that you want to develop, at least to some degree. If you aren't motivated enough to get your butt into the office at a set time every morning, you have a serious leadership problem. You will never lead an army if you can't even lead yourself. People are watching you constantly—employees, clients, and fellow entrepreneurs. And they are deciding whether or not they want to work with you and follow your example.

Leroy Eims wrote, "A leader is one who sees more than others see, who sees farther than others see, and who sees before others do." It's not easy being a leader because you need to balance optimism and realism, intuition and planning, faith and fact. That means getting to know yourself and having confidence in your abilities, as well as seeing your weaknesses and areas of lack.

In the organization of Jehovah's Witnesses, everyone is expected to take the lead. Although they defer to male leadership and headship, when a man is not around, a woman is expected to organize, lead, conduct and teach. A young man is constantly encouraged to work towards becoming an elder in the congregation and will move through the ranks as a ministerial servant before becoming an elder. Leadership qualities are taught regularly at the meetings and the examples of leaders such as King David, King Solomon, and Jesus Christ are used as models of powerful leaders.

You may not be a leader naturally. But to grow your business, you do need to take the lead.

Question to Ponder:
Do you take the lead in
your business or are you
somehow waiting for it to
happen automatically?

Support One Another

Johann Wolfgang von Goethe wrote, "Treat people as if they were what they ought to be and help them become what they are capable of being." In other words, *support one another to greatness.*

Just the other day, I read in a newsletter that a social club in Vancouver was sponsoring an evening of drinks and appetizers, with all proceeds going to help out a neighboring business that had been vandalized and needed some expensive repairs. My heart sang as I thought about one business supporting another. It felt so right, and my opinion of that social club went through the roof. I know that they didn't do it based on how I would feel about them; they did it because it obviously felt right—but I thoroughly applauded their initiative of support for another business.

You may have an employee who needs some support through a tough time. It may be your business partner who needs assistance. One of your clients may be experiencing a challenge, and you can come to their aid in a way that is extraordinary and unexpected.

In a world made up of entrepreneurs working out of their home offices, solopreneurs with no one around to connect with on a daily basis, and many small enterprises struggling to get their feet on solid ground, a feeling of support can mean a tremendous amount.

It could be as simple as sending a card to show you are thinking about someone, or as costly as giving an employee a week off with pay to deal with a serious illness or death in the family.

It's one of the reasons that people appreciate the community of Jehovah's Witnesses. If someone is in the hospital, it will be announced at the meeting so people can phone, visit or send a card. During the years that my aged mother was not able to attend the meetings physically, the congregation supported her by connecting her into the meeting via phone. It was a highlight of her week to feel supported by the congregation.

You don't have to move mountains to help people feel supported. You can pick up the phone and let somebody know you are thinking about them, send an article or news item to a client that pertains to their business with a short note, or send flowers to a client who is in the hospital or had a personal tragedy.

Supporting others is pivotal to your long-term success. Building relationships, community and that ever expanding circle of trust with people will bring back results tenfold. Take a few minutes every day and support someone. You'll be glad you did!

"Treat people as if they were what they ought to be and help them become what they are capable of being."

Follow Up

I f you don't want a Jehovah's Witness to call back on you regularly, you better not accept any literature, engage in conversation or be too, too nice—because they'll be back! Their follow-up is impeccable. Is yours?

There is a saying in network marketing: "The fortune is in the follow-up." Yet so many of us let potential clients slip through our fingers because we never make that phone call, never send that email or don't send the brochure. We get busy, **we** decide **they** aren't really interested, or we lose their contact information. Happens to the best of us!

If you do choose to speak with a JW at your door, they will leave your home and write down in their Return Visit book, your address, name, the conversation highlights, any scriptures read from the Bible, what they left you in the form of a book, magazine, or brochure, and when they promised to return. Then when they do follow-up and speak with you, they will review their notes, have the conversation, and note the details again. It also gets counted as a Return Visit on that slip they fill out about their preaching work activity that month. So it is all very organized and documented. It is also well-rehearsed, as they practice making return visits, following up with people and taking your interest to the next level at their meetings. They take it seriously because they believe your life is at risk of being destroyed.

What can you learn from the kind of diligence, organization, planning and thought that goes into their follow-up? If they can be that serious about pursuing any bit of interest, what are you doing about possible interest in your business?

What systems do you have in place for follow-up? You may be efficient in getting your message out, but could the effectiveness be improved through better follow-up? It has been said that people need to hear a message seven times before they actually respond. Do you have different methods for follow-up? Throwing your message out once in awhile with no follow-through or consistency is a waste of energy, time and money!

The fortune is in the follow-up. Networking marketing companies know it and the JWs know it. Do **you** know it? Perhaps more importantly, what are you **doing** about it? Improve your follow-up and your business can't help but grow. Seriously!

Success Secret #87	Know Your Rights

You can't defend rights that you don't know. It doesn't mean you have to become a lawyer anytime soon, but you should know some basic rights you have in running your business.

Do you know what is legal and not legal with regards to sending emails? Do you know what you can legally write off as expenses against your business income? Are you aware of copyright laws when you submit an article to a magazine?

One of the biggest mistakes I see with many entrepreneurs is the lack of seriousness they take in running a business. Because so much of our business takes place in the virtual world, it affords us a measure of security, of perceived anonymity, and a feeling of being protected—a feeling that may or may not be accurate.

If you are operating a retail store, a restaurant, or an office, you need to know your rights when it comes to contracts, by-laws and municipal regulations. You'd better know your rights before you sign on the dotted line! Once your signature is on a piece of paper, that is a binding contract. You can be in serious trouble if you have agreed to do something you cannot live up to.

In Canada, Jehovah's Witnesses know that it is their right to come to your front door with their message. You may not like it, but it is their right. However, it is not their right to enter your backyard. That becomes trespassing. They will defend their right to preach, but they also know the limitations of their rights. They have an entire legal department with some very powerful, successful lawyers on board who just deal with legal issues for their organization.

Do you have a lawyer to consult with on various aspects of your business? Do you check things out, or do you "wing it," assuming that all is well? Not knowing what your rights are can cost you time, money and reputation. That can be extremely serious. So take the time to know your rights. It will distinguish you as a business that is serious about being around for the long term.

"Not knowing what your rights are can cost you time, money and reputation."

*Success
Secret
#88*   Continue Learning

Your business is growing. Finally—all that hard work is paying off, and you are thrilled. You're running to keep up, but boy it feels good to have a thriving business. No time for more workshops, teleclasses, you haven't read a book in months (until this one, of course!) and you let go of your coach because everything is going so well.

Hold your horses please! If this describes you in any way, shape or form, this chapter may be the most important one in the book.

Continuous learning is so important. You can't just stop learning any more than you can stop eating or drinking or sleeping. Learning in business is what will keep you up-to-date, on top of things and continually motivated and inspired to improve. Stagnation in your own education will spill over to your business. Guaranteed!

You may stop learning because there just isn't any more time in a day. Then find time. Rather than watching an hour of television in the evening, listen to a teleclass instead. Don't listen to the radio in the car as you drive to an appointment; choose an instructional, motivational, inspiring CD instead. Cancel the newspaper during the week and, instead, spend thirty minutes reading a good business book. Indulge in the newspaper as a weekend treat.

I can't tell you how many times I read through the Bible during the years I was a JW and still learned something new! It would amaze you how many articles I read on the same subject over and over and over again. Just when I thought, "What new publication can they possibly come up with this year," one would be released!

I lived in an environment of constant learning. Jehovah's Witnesses are one of the largest publishers of religious materials in the world, and their people are bombarded with learning every day of their lives.

Today in my business, I learn constantly. Technology alone is changing daily. Do you know what Technorati is? Is "blog" a foreign word in your vocabulary? Does "podcasting" sound like a new kind of fishing equipment? You really need to know what is happening in technology, because times are changing and quickly. What worked today is not going to work tomorrow, and many people will be left wondering what happened!

Find the time to continue your business and personal education. Otherwise, the windfall you are enjoying today may not last, and you can be caught unawares because you were just too busy enjoying your success to keep up with change!

*"Learning in business is
what will keep you up-to-date,
on top of things and
continually motivated and
inspired to improve."*

The Tortoise or the Hare

S ome entrepreneurs come out of the starting gate with a bang. They are off and running and there's no stopping them. Everybody is talking about them, they make headline news, sales (and expenses) are soaring, and every entrepreneur is wondering why they can't be more like them! However, because there was no planning, no systems, and no structure, they soon fall off to the side and quit—exhausted, depleted and broke.

Meanwhile, another entrepreneur takes her time, building slowly but solidly. Small growth year by year, good solid relationships, amazing systems in place and a rock-solid reputation in the industry are her earmarks of success. She doesn't make front page news, but she has a business she can sell, that pays her well, and that she can walk away from for weekends and holidays every year.

Which one are you? It's wonderful to have stupendous growth; there's nothing wrong with being in the news; being the leader in the industry can work in your favor. But can you sustain it and continue to build?

Incremental growth that is measurable, sustainable and duplicable is what long-term success is all about.

Twenty-five years ago, there were almost two million Jehovah's Witnesses. Today there are almost seven million. Not bad growth for 25 years. Nothing earth-shattering, but definitely sustainable.

We've all seen network marketing companies come on the scene, make a splash, lure some big names away from other companies, and subsequently fizzle and die. What happened? Picture a six-legged table. It's strong, it's secure, it's solid. Now picture a spinning top revolving on one axis. What happens when it stops spinning? It falls over. Why? Because it only had one foot on the ground.

What about your business?

Marketing gurus teach that to be sustainable, you need to grow various legs of your business. So let's say you are a coach. Private coaching is one leg of your business. However, that leg is limited by the number of hours a day you can personally work and the limit of days in the week. So you need another leg.

Perhaps you have a book or CD that is another leg. Not everyone who buys your book or CDs will hire you as a coach so that leg has unlimited possibilities. Maybe you add a leg of a workshop where you teach an entire group methods and philosophies that are the foundation of your private work. Another leg could be a weekend retreat or full week cruise. Perhaps you add other products that you didn't produce but are great complements to your practice and would benefit your clients. So you now have affiliates, and whenever someone buys their product off your website, at your workshop or as a personal client, you get paid. And your sixth leg could be a training manual to help other coaches build a similar business.

Do you see how much more solid that would be than just depending on personal coaching as your only source of income?

This system will not happen overnight—trust me! But if you focus on one leg, get it solid, work on the next, get it solid, work on the next, get it solid—do you see how you could build yourself a very nice business? Every business can do this.

You may be the tortoise, plodding along, doing your thing, feeling a bit dejected with the speed that you are growing your business as the hare flies by and makes you feel inadequate. However, steady growth in the short term will work well for you in the long term— and the long term is what counts. Being a flash in the pan is fun for the moment but has no sustainability.

Success Secret #90

Stay Humble

I'm fascinated by how many really successful entrepreneurs talk about humility. Once I tuned into that word, I was amazed by the number of times it came up in books, teleclasses or workshops. Humility is really, really important in growing your business. What is it exactly? It is defined as "a modest opinion or estimate of one's own importance or rank; lowliness, meekness, submissiveness."

Entrepreneurs will often struggle with their businesses because they are afraid of asking for help. *What will people think? Won't I look stupid?* I recently worked with a woman who came out of a corporate setting. She was absolutely stunned that on a conference call I said, "I don't know how to use that technology. I'll need some help figuring it out." She told me later that she had never heard anyone in a leadership position be so honest about not knowing something. I was stunned that she came from an environment where saying, "I don't know" is not encouraged and is possibly even condemned.

How are you ever supposed to learn anything, if you are supposed to already know it all? That's a mighty awkward position to be in!

Being humble means knowing you will never know it all so you have your eyes and ears open to learn more. Staying humble is about remaining approachable and meek, as opposed to haughty, proud and arrogant. You may be the boss, you may own the company and you may run the show, but if you walk around like you are above everyone else, you may find yourself very much alone!

As missionaries in Ecuador, I had an amazing opportunity to practice humility. As the foreigners, my husband and I were put in a place of reverence and honor just by virtue of the color of our skin, our language, our decades of experience as Jehovah's Witnesses and our economic situation. How could we help these people if they practically bowed in front of us? Many of them also came straight out of the Catholic religion, where kissing rings, kneeling and bowing, and worshiping their religious authorities were common practices.

I knew there were things they needed to learn from us, so I had to be a teacher. I taught village women about birth control, I taught some how to read and write better, I helped them learn how to discipline their children to sit at a meeting at the Kingdom Hall, and I taught them how to preach to their neighbors. They humbly learned, and it was beautiful to see.

They were amazing farmers and gardeners. In one village, we lived on about a quarter of an acre and had a large plot set aside for gardening. As we were on the equator, we could grow vegetables all year round. So I asked them to teach me how to plant local produce, how to fertilize using natural products such as guinea pig manure which was prevalent in the village, and how to cook some of their local dishes. They blossomed as teachers as our roles were reversed for those learning sessions. I became the student, and a very humble one at that, as I was also dealing with learning a foreign language!

Humility—the ability to say, "I don't know, but I'm willing to learn"—will transform your business. It will keep you approachable to your clients and employees. Your peers will not feel intimidated. You will be much better liked. Arrogance, pride and intimidation are all earmarks of fear disguised. Bottom line, there are ways you show that you don't believe you are good enough at some level. We all have gifts and we all have areas of lack. By showing up with your gifts, teaching them, helping and supporting others, you allow others to show up with their gifts where you lack.

Humility is like oil to a machine. It will stop tempers from flaring up, keep people feeling appreciated and supported, and keep everybody in a learning and growing curve in your business. It may feel old-fashioned or out-of-date to talk about humility in business, but it works. It really does!

Be Generous

Are you a generous person? I'm not just talking about money, but about everything in life. Are you generous with your knowledge, resources, time and money? You will be amazed at what happens in your life when you are generous. There's a Bible scripture that many people know: *There is more happiness in giving than there is in receiving.* There's a lot of happiness in receiving too, but giving definitely has its perks. So ask yourself: Am I a generous person?

No one wants to think of themselves as a Scrooge—that's for sure. But you just may be a Scrooge wearing Santa's costume. Time is precious and so is money. You obviously need to think carefully about where you spend it—but are you tight-fisted or openhearted? I love the dictionary definition of generous as "being free from meanness or smallness of mind or character." As you can see from that definition, generosity goes far beyond money. It includes our whole way of thinking and being.

Jehovah's Witnesses do not pass a collection plate at their meetings. No collection is ever taken. There is a box at the back of the Kingdom Hall where people can make a donation—anonymously, if they wish, or in exchange for a tax receipt. There is no obligation, but each month there is a financial statement read for the congregation. It will outline the bills, the contributions received and the balance in the bank. So everyone is aware of the income and output. There are talks on meeting the expenses of the congregation and on having a generous spirit. But at the end of the day, there is no accounting for money contributed on an individual basis. But each year, the organization receives sufficient money to operate an international organization.

Generosity is a quality that a successful entrepreneur wants to incorporate into his or her business. Think about how you can support your community, reward your employees, bonus your best clients or give to a great cause. If you are thinking of giving in your business you put yourself into the energetic flow of money. Even the word "currency" indicates movement or circulation. So be part of the circulation of money on the planet and bless it coming into your business and moving out to do good work on the planet. Stop the critical circulation of money and you may find the dam you have created in your business backfires on you in interesting ways.

Generosity is a critical part of the energetic flow of abundance and prosperity in your life. You may give a little or a lot, but whatever you give will come back to you tenfold!

Success Secret #92	Be Flexible

This may seem like a total contradiction to what I have said about being resolute and convicted in your belief. However, you need to have a flexibility that doesn't detract from your resoluteness and conviction. Does that seem almost impossible?

Whenever I think of flexibility, I think of the bamboo plant. Amidst death and destruction, it was bamboo that survived the Hiroshima atomic blast closer to ground zero than any other living thing. Its resistance to breaking under tension is superior to steel. Did you know that Thomas Edison successfully used a carbonized bamboo filament in his experiment with the first light bulb? He also used bamboo as rebar for the reinforcement of his swimming pool. Similarly, Alexander Graham Bell made use of bamboo for his first phonograph needle. From the most delicate uses to the most sturdy, the flexibility of bamboo enables it to adapt to many different situations.

People's inability to know when to be flexible and when to stand resolute costs them dearly in business and in life. One of the lessons that I learned very well as a JW was the timing of my flexibility. If you ask any Jehovah's Witness if they will go to war, celebrate Christmas, take blood or vote in an election, they will unequivocally tell you "no." Those are decisions made on their values, on their belief system and on their principles. They won't budge, even if they lose out economically, are tortured, or die because of their decision.

But listen to a JW who is experienced and well trained speaking with someone at their door and you will see a flexibility that is quite remarkable. They will know remarkably well when to not make an issue out of something that is irrelevant, when to agree, and how to bring people around to a line of reasoning.

When I entered my business in the automotive industry some years ago, my salespeople were stunned as they watched me "dance the dance" with some pretty chauvinistic, difficult men in the car business. I instinctively knew when to be firm, when to joke with them and let them know I was actually fun to deal with in business, when to give in to their demands, and when to ask for the order—all done through the well honed practice of flexibility!

Decide where you are not willing to be flexible and where you can bend. Nothing frustrates customers more than when there is no rule-bending to accommodate their request.

I listened to a phone conversation the other day where the sales-person kept harping on about the rules and policies. My friend was irate, as she knew it was a simple thing to fix, but the inflexibility of the salesperson left her absolutely frustrated and not wanting to ever do business with that company again. Nordstrom in the States has earned an amazing reputation for customer service because they are very flexible in their return policy. I personally try to avoid buying clothes without a return policy, especially if I paid full price. Neither is right or wrong. Just know that your flexibility or lack of it in business will affect your bottom line—guaranteed.

Question to Ponder:
Where do you need to be
flexible in your business?

Be Genuine

"Nobody cares how much you know until they know how much you care." So said Theodore Roosevelt. Isn't that the truth? You can have a salesperson rattle off the data to you like a computer, and you won't buy because they're insincere. You may meet someone highly intelligent but who appears officious and aloof. You don't want to do business with them.

"Genuine" is a hard characteristic to specifically define because it is open to interpretation. Today fake fur looks as real as the real thing. Fake leather is incredibly close to genuine leather. Phoniness can't always be spotted in someone immediately. It's sometimes only the test of time that shows up a person's insincerity.

One of the things that JWs definitely work on is being genuine. As they live and breathe their religious beliefs, they work at incorporating them into their everyday life. They do not just show up on Sunday morning, listen to a talk, and then go out and have an affair, lie and cheat on their taxes and run over the neighbor's dog who kept them up barking! They will stop and help the neighbor with a task, they will carry an older person's groceries for them, and they will give you back the money if you give them the wrong change.

In business, you really want to be genuine. It's important to come across as sincere and honest and upright, but if those aren't qualities that come straight from your heart, the hypocrisy will show up, sometimes at the darndest times! Under pressure, the real person will show up. Put a little stress in your life and that's when you find out what you are really made of. If those values just look good on paper, they won't show up when a competitor is spreading nasty rumors or you just lost your biggest client to the new kid on the block.

Counterfeit money is big business. But at the end of the day, it's not worth the paper it's printed on. It's only the genuine stuff that will last. Same in your business. Be genuine, and if you aren't happy with what genuine looks like for you, work on it some more.

"Nobody cares how much you know until they know how much you care."

Success Secret #94

Use Your Words to Encourage

Eleanor Roosevelt said, "Great minds discuss ideas; average minds discuss events; small minds discuss people." What do you discuss? Do you gossip? Do you say nasty things? How encouraging are you to be around?

The Bible says: "As apples of gold in silver carvings is a word spoken at the right time for it." Our words can cut like a knife, they can pierce the heart of another, and they can heal and soothe. What effect do you want your words to have? If they are like apples of gold in silver carvings, they are highly valuable and much esteemed.

People today are, for the most part, beaten down. They are discouraged, depressed and don't often feel very good about themselves. Use of anti-depressants is at an all-time high, and those who don't take them often think they should! Employers are stressed and are taking it out on their employees. Demands on everyone's time is high, and despite all the modern conveniences, there seems to be less time than ever. People are putting in longer hours, sitting in horrible rush hour traffic and yet have less to show for it than ever before. They are feeling the stress and strain of life.

You have the ability to completely change that for someone today!

So how effective are you at using your words to encourage those around you? Are you empowering—or are you right in there complaining and bitching and moaning and groaning about everything from the weather to the unfair taxes to the government to your ungrateful clients! Even the dog can't do anything right!

People will be attracted to someone who is positive and who speaks positively. They will hang on to your empowering message like water in the desert. They will read your newsletters, they will attend your workshops, and they will want to do business with you.

Encouraging words need not be flattery or insincere compliments. Encouragement means to build up, edify, recommend and inspire.

Probably because the Bible has a lot to say about encouragement, I was encouraged to encourage. It was a way of life to think about those less fortunate, to make a phone call and say hi to someone who was sick, or to give a friend a hug when you saw them, because you really cared. For a JW, the congregation is like a family, and encouragement is the predominant energy in a family that is healthy and thriving.

To this day, I try to be encouraging. It's why I love coaching and teaching—it's all about encouragement. But business is really about encouraging others. Your clients will appreciate a kind word, your employees will shine if you praise them in earnest, and your family will support you much more in your entrepreneurial endeavors if you encourage them as they encourage you.

What goes around comes around—and with encouragement, that is definitely the truth. Because I encourage others, I know that I can pick up the phone and speak with any one of my friends and be encouraged by them. Also, by encouraging others and seeing them glow with their possibilities, it encourages me.

If you have a plant that lacks water, pretty soon the leaves fade and wither. It looks pitiful very quickly. So what happens when you give it some water? Sometimes you can literally see it come back to life before your eyes. The leaves perk up, it starts to grow new ones— you've given it a whole new opportunity to live with a little bit of water. Your words of encouragement can be like that water. You can create in your business a positive energy of growth, optimism and support just by your words of encouragement. You're that powerful!

Success Secret #95

Be Conversational

Conversation is a dialogue. That means that it is a two-sided conversation. Many people seem to forget that as they unleash their verbal diarrhea. They literally blab about their products, service or business, and you cannot get a word in edgewise. You could be a wall for all they care, as they go on and on and on and on about themselves. Have you ever been subjected to that kind of so-called conversation and wondered how to politely excuse yourself from the person? Or have *you* ever been guilty of *being* that person?

Conversation means an *interchange* of thoughts. Another definition of conversation is social intercourse. The words, interchange and intercourse would indicate two things in my mind—you both need to be participating. However, conversations can often be one-sided, and if you are the one on the receiving end, you can feel unheard, unnoticed, talked at rather than spoken with, angry, and resentful. You very quickly shut out the words and stop listening.

From a business point of view, this is serious! You definitely don't want your clients or your employees doing any of the above.

It is sometimes called the "art of conversation" because it is a skill or an art that needs to be cultivated. You may need to work at conversation. How does it work? You need to ask questions and then listen. You share and then you listen. You acknowledge and then you listen. Notice the one word that keeps showing up: *listen*. It has been said we have two ears and one mouth for a reason. We are encouraged to listen twice as much as we speak!

How's your art of conversation?

I bet you're not the least bit surprised that JWs are trained in the art of conversation. They practice having upbuilding, encouraging, informative conversations. They are aware of their conversation and try to ensure that it is cheerful, warm, sincere and appropriate to the person they are speaking with. They would not have the same conversation with a Muslim as they would with an atheist.

Are you that versatile in your conversation? Can you become more adaptable and flexible to the interests of the person you are having a conversation with?

For example, if your client is an avid hang glider and that client brings several thousands of dollars worth of business into your company every year, do you think you might want to find out something about hang gliding? If the vast majority of your clients are from a certain country, would you want to learn something about it? Show an interest, ask questions, share a story, or watch the news for what interests them and then incorporate those tidbits of information into your conversation with them. They will feel appreciated by you and valued in your conversation.

Just because you can open your mouth and words can come out, that does not mean that you have the art of conversation down pat with no room for improvement. Become a witness to your conversation, and start to notice whether you interrupt people in mid-sentence, whether you really listen to them without thinking about what you want to say while they are talking, and see how many questions you really do ask. You may be better or worse than you really think you are. You may never have even thought about the art of conversation. It's a good time to start thinking about what is coming out of your mouth and whether you are using your words to the greatest effect!

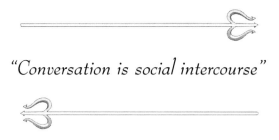

"Conversation is social intercourse"

Success Secret #96

Follow Rules

There are times to follow the rules and times to break them. When do you want to follow the rules? When it comes to anything legal or to do with taxes, you want to follow the rules. You absolutely, definitely, positively, want to comply with legal and tax rules. The penalties are far too severe for breaking those rules.

It doesn't mean that you can't hire a great accountant who knows the areas of income tax. I highly recommend you get the most leverage for being an entrepreneur from an accounting standpoint. Use every tax write-off available to you and be conscientious about saving your receipts and keeping accurate records for your bookkeeper and accountant.

However, you don't want to be messing with not submitting taxes that you collect on behalf of the government when they ask for it. That is one area where you want to follow the rules EXPLICITLY! I cannot stress this enough. Too many entrepreneurs have found themselves caught in a really serious situation because they procrastinated or avoided certain situations that involve the government and money—to their detriment.

I am a natural rule breaker. Tell me to go left and I immediately want to go right. I have a belief that I would rather ask for forgiveness than permission. However, I learned from the example of the JWs that you follow certain rules that are important to your safety and protection and are mandatory from a legal point of view.

On the other hand, there were rules that were not followed. For example, I snuck into some apartment buildings and dodged care-takers as I tried to reach as many people as possible before being thrown out of the building or asked to leave. In that case, JWs will usually see "saving the life" of the tenant as more important than the rule against soliciting. They will also not vote or go to war even if the rules say they must—and they pay the consequences, even if that means imprisonment, torture or death.

You will have to decide for yourself according to your values and principles where and when you will follow the rules and when you will follow your own path. But please, please, please, in the area of taxes, follow the rules. It's pretty tough to run a business from jail!

Devil With A Briefcase

Success Secret #97 — Utilize Your Resources

D o you make good use of your resources? Those can include time and money—but what about your joint venture partners, affiliates, products, and services? Are you utilizing them to their fullest potential?

Here's an example to think about. Jehovah's Witnesses will often share a Kingdom Hall with other congregations. Because they like to keep their congregations at a certain size to ensure that people don't get "lost" in a congregation that is too big, they will split and form two congregations.

Consequently, they will have two or even more congregations using the one Kingdom Hall. What a bonus! Expenses are now divided amongst the congregations and so is the workload of maintenance and upkeep. It also means that the resource, the Kingdom Hall, is being fully utilized with sometimes as many as four meetings happening on a Sunday, and it is now used every night of the week.

What about your business? I know of one chiropractor's office that allowed someone holding a workshop to use their facility on the weekend when they weren't seeing clients. Now they had money coming in on the weekend that normally wouldn't have been in their budget.

Perhaps you have a great joint venture partner with a product that you promote. They are easy to work with, give excellent service, and your clients love their product. Have you checked into whether or not they have other products that could also be promoted? If you have a database and clientele that you are offering a number of services and products to, are you offering them everything possible?

Let's say you are a massage therapist doing massages for your clients. Can you possibly offer additional products or services to your clients, thereby more fully utilizing the resource of having a number of clients? Perhaps you could offer an aromatherapy line, or a manicure or pedicure service. You don't even have to do it—you just need to make it available to your clients. You may not even need to stock it—you may simply direct people to another service and get a referral fee when you do so. That is utilizing your resources fully. I'll bet there is some unmined gold in your business when you start to think of more fully utilizing your resources!

Question to Ponder:
Where can you make
better use of resources in
your business?

Make Sacrifices
When Necessary

A re you willing to make sacrifices to grow your business? One of the most amazing things I watch with many entrepreneurs is their level of entitlement. They expect to have it all with very little work. I've had people phone me wanting to earn $150,000 a year when they haven't even made $25,000 yet—and they'll tell me that, by the way, they don't want to work too hard! They are doomed to failure in their business and in their life. When did the concept of hard work and sacrifice disappear? The age of entitlement has many entrepreneurs living in a fairytale land that does not exist. Sorry, hard work may have gone out of style, but it is very real in a successful entrepreneur's career.

What kind of sacrifice am I referring to? Obviously, I'm not talking about going up to some mountaintop with your child and tying him to an altar with a knife in your hand. That's a popular Bible story of Abraham and Isaac, but it does indicate the level of discomfort certain habits and ways of thinking may entail in your life.

Perhaps you need to make some financial sacrifices to grow your business. Maybe you can't do the expensive family vacation this year because you purchased some new equipment for your business that will help take it to new levels of profitability next year. Maybe you work Saturday mornings on your book as uninterrupted time rather than sleeping in or golfing. You may need to make some time sacrifices for your business's sake. Watching television every night may need to be replaced with reading business books or taking a class once a week.

JWs are thoroughly indoctrinated about making sacrifices. As they are so programmed to be focused on surviving Armageddon and living in a paradise world forever, they are willing to make massive sacrifices. They may sacrifice by not buying a home or not having children so they can keep their life simple and focused on their service to God. Those are big sacrifices to make for an intangible of living forever in a paradise right here on earth. However, I made those sacrifices willingly as did many of my friends at the time.

The JWs' example of sacrifice teaches something very important for every entrepreneur.

You will only make the sacrifice
if you think the reward is great enough.

I thought of having a child that had every quality I didn't like in my own family and every quality that I didn't like in my husband's family (and there were plenty of them), and all of a sudden the idea of having a perfect child in paradise became a pretty awesome reward for a relatively small sacrifice. Looking back, of course, that decision represents a whole different level of sacrifice as I have no children and no prospect of having perfect children on a paradise earth, either!

So ask yourself: Are you willing to make sacrifices to grow your business? What is the reward for making those sacrifices? Is the reward great enough in your mind to warrant those sacrifices? If not, then you need a bigger WHY.

Question to Ponder:
Are you realistic about the
sacrifices you need to make to
achieve your business goals?

Success Secret #99

Have All of Your Materials Ready

Have you ever watched someone do a sales presentation and they were missing a file, a contract, or even something as simple as a pen? Seems fairly simple when you are an experienced entrepreneur, doesn't it? Maybe so, and maybe not.

Sometimes the most experienced of entrepreneurs become almost cavalier in their business because they have done it so many times. A new entrepreneur may be the one more inclined to check his briefcase ten times, be at the presentation 30 minutes early to check the equipment before he speaks, and have the contract in the hands of the potential client a day early. On the other hand, when you have done something a thousand times before, you can become nonchalant and offhanded, failing to give the situation the attention it deserves.

JWs actually have skits in which someone knocks on a door and then opens her briefcase to pull out a magazine, only to have the whole thing fall open and everything spill at the doorstep. I remember one time in particular when I pulled a *Watchtower* and *Awake* out of my

briefcase while at someone's home. Because my briefcase wasn't as well organized as it should have been, as I pulled out the *Awake*, the whole front cover of the magazine ripped off. I was pretty embarrassed as I tried not to burst out laughing!

JWs are also taught to have their materials neat and clean. They may have a "study" Bible where everything is marked up and underlined and cross-notes are in the margins. That is NOT the Bible they are instructed to take from door-to-door. Why not? They appreciate that many people they speak with will see the Bible as a very holy book that should not be defaced in any way, and that the underlines and marking could be distracting to someone as you read a scripture to them.

Not at Home slips, their Return Visit Book to take notes in, literature in various languages that they frequently encounter as they go from door-to-door, their Bible, and a writing tool are all standard items in any JW's briefcase. They have their materials ready.

Can you be that organized? Absolutely! Can you be that prepared? With some planning, for sure! Think through your next presentation, workshop or event and make sure you have all of your materials ready. The image you will portray to your potential clients, employees or peers will be one of professionalism and caring enough to do an absolutely fabulous job.

Question to Ponder:
Is there an area of having
your materials ready that
you can improve on in
your business?

Success Secret #100	Go Above and Beyond

I n a world where doing the minimum is considered acceptable and even desirable, going above and beyond may not come naturally. You may be looking at ways to slack off, do less, create passive income, automate your business and get by with the least amount of effort.

I'm not knocking passive income or automating your business, but if your motive in business is to scrape by in the effort category, you may want to reevaluate a few things.

Everyone naturally wants the most amount of money for the least amount of effort. But it is those businesses that go above and beyond that see HUGE results in their bottom line. People today expect the worst while hoping for the best. You may be the same. You go into the grocery store on a weekend and you expect long line-ups and crowded aisles, yet you hope that everybody did their shopping during the week and that every cashier is open for business. Am I right? I rarely wait in line at the grocery store and am so grateful that they have lots of cashiers available and most of the registers open. They even recently replaced all of their debit machines so my debit card goes through quickly every time. Although it is a discount grocery store, and part of a massive chain, they actually do a better job of service than some of the higher-end stores I visit for specialty items. They go above and beyond, and I appreciate it.

Going above and beyond may simply mean offering your clients a good cup of coffee, having a bowl of candies for them to help themselves to, having enough parking so it's easy to visit you, having a real live voice on the other end of the phone instead of a machine, giving extra bonuses and value for your service or following up when it wasn't part of the deal. People will appreciate it because they aren't expecting it but they sure are hoping for it.

JWs are taught to go above and beyond. Quite honestly, part of their motivation is because they are reporting everything they do in their preaching activity at the end of the month, so going above and beyond may not be completely altruistic. Consequently, visiting someone interested in their message in the hospital or bringing a book or special item of interest to your home may be a combination of being of service and meeting their monthly quota. However, it's not much different than a business that goes above and beyond, knowing that such services or extra value will affect their bottom line.

In a world where everybody is doing the minimum to scrape by, try doing one extra thing for your clients this month and see the effect. What can you do? This morning I just taught a teleclass. I mentioned a free ebook from someone that I really enjoyed. Rather than have everybody have to go and search for the person and the ebook, I simply sent it out with my notes and recording on the call as an extra bonus. I went above and beyond. Immediately I received three emails of appreciation for the call and one further inquiry into my other services. I didn't do that simple thing for any recognition or monetary benefit. I just try to always go above and beyond. It's a habit in my life that I learned from the JWs, and it has served me well in my business life.

Going above and beyond is one area where you can stand out from the masses. Think about how you can go above and beyond in little ways and see how your value stands head and shoulders above the rest. That's a very profitable place to be.

"Going above and beyond is one area where you can stand out from the masses."

Success Secret #101

Pee or Get off the Pot

I think those words were some of my Mom's favorite words while I was growing up. She meant *make up your mind*. Today I watch entrepreneurs struggle with decision making, not moving ahead because they are so afraid of making a bad decision. As a result, they live in a place of analysis paralysis. *What if I make the wrong decision? What if I fail? What if something bad happens?* And so they sit on the fence in a place of inactivity.

The only guaranteed result of sitting on that fence is a sore rear end! Action, right or wrong, is necessary in business. Momentum is a good thing—and momentum comes from taking a first step. Without activity, your business will dry up and die. *"But what if..."* you ask, thinking of everything that could go wrong.

Think of everything that you do as a "no-lose decision". You WIN no matter what happens. I look at it this way. For 38 years, I waited for the end of the world. It didn't happen and I moved on. But those were 38 amazing years of training, discipline and focus. I had 18 happy years of marriage. I spent four years as a missionary in an incredible country. Wow! I won every step of the way. There were plenty of losses, too, of course, but I don't even let my mind go to those, because the wins completely offset them.

Every decision you make has the potential to be negative or positive. It's your choice. Decide what you want in your life and go get it. If you want to be a best-selling author, start writing. If you want to be a Hollywood actor, start taking acting lessons. If you want to be the next Martha Stewart, start growing your business. Decide first in your mind who you are and then act like it. "**Be** who you want to be, then **Do** what they would do, and you'll **Have** what they have" is a good motto for life.

The JWs actually refer to their religion as the Truth with a capital "T". That's how convinced they are that they are right. Imagine talking about having the Truth every day of your life. You'd start to believe it, don't you think? And of course they do, with every fiber of their being.

What do you believe about you? Decide who you are. See yourself as it. Then go get it. My Mom's words have stuck with me and I live them. I move forward constantly. Sometimes I make mistakes—but who hasn't? Sometimes I have to retrace my steps. Oh well! Sometimes I realize that I could have done better. So what? I'm sure I could have found a better editor, a better illustrator, a better printer, for this book. I'm sure that I could have—if I spent days, weeks, months, or even years analyzing this project to death! And that's precisely what would have happened: it would have died a very non-spectacular death, along with a dozen other projects that never came to fruition because I couldn't make up my mind.

I am passionate about this because I see entrepreneurs stagnating in their businesses all the time. When I started my pole dancing business, many women who bought a business from me told me they'd THOUGHT about doing something similar but hadn't acted on it. They had the idea or concept but sat on the fence and analyzed it to death. So rather than being in a position to sell me a business, they were buying one from me. Which side of that coin would you rather be on?

You can't lose. You can only WIN. I have learned so much from the amazing people I have worked with on this book. They have been supportive, fun and incredible to work with. That's a WIN. Could I have found people more supportive, more fun, more knowledgeable? Perhaps. But why go there? The ones I found worked and worked well. Done. Finished. Completed. I peed and got off the pot. Sitting there all day is not productive, not particularly enjoyable, and you will end up with a sore rear end. Make decisions. Take a "can't Lose, can only Win" approach. Pee and get off the pot! You'll really be glad you did.

Wait...
there's more!

If you would like to receive three bonus chapters please go to www.devilwithabriefcase.com and click on Bonus Chapters. You will be asked for a password in order to login.

The password is the title of Secret #25.

You will receive three bonus chapters and an extra-special gift I've prepared just for you.

I'd also love to hear your feedback and comments about *Devil with a Briefcase*. So go to
www.devilwithabriefcase.com
now and click on Bonus Chapters.

To your outrageous success!

Jan

Learn more about How to Become a Successful Spiritual Entrepreneur.

Still Looking for Your Passion and Gifts?

If you are stuck right at the beginning of the entrepreneurial journey, wondering what gifts, talents and passions you possess, check out the CDs on *Identifying Your Sacred Gifts and Finding Your Passion, Discovering the Winner, Warrior and Wizard in You.*

Are You Really an Entrepreneur?

Questioning if you have the qualities, the necessary focus and discipline, and the passion to become an entrepreneur? Those are good questions to ask BEFORE you embark on the journey. I have prepared a very thought-provoking CD called: *Do You Have What it Takes to Be an Entrepreneur?*

Do you struggle with the Left-Brain side of Entrepreneurship?

If you're stuck with Systems, Schedules and Business Planning, you're perfectly normal! Most entrepreneurs struggle with these areas of their business. Let me help you! *Getting it Together – Left-Brain Details for the Right-Brain Entrepreneur* CD is all about systems, time management, setting up your business, the easiest business plan in the world that will excite you and other ways to make running your business easy and fun.

Does the Emotional Rollercoaster of Entrepreneurship have you coming and going?

Many entrepreneurs aren't accustomed to dealing with the ups and downs of being in business for themselves. How do you handle them easily and gracefully? What do you need as C.O.O. of your business? Who do you have to be personally in order to succeed professionally?

Learn how to be outrageously successful in your business with the two-CD set: *Who Are You? Getting to Know the C.O.O. of Your Business,* where you'll learn what it takes to be the best in your business while enjoying life!

Is Selling a Struggle for You or Something You Avoid at all Costs?

If you hate selling the old-fashioned, pushy, put your foot in the door way, you will love *Heart to Heart Selling – Selling that Makes Everyone Feel Good*. This two-CD set is a very different perspective on "cold-calling", objections and building relationships in business. You'll actually learn to like yourself in sales and look forward to sharing your message with others.

**These and more Spiritual Entrepreneur
Resources available online at:
www.spiritualentrepreneurinfo.com**

Speaking Engagements

A top notch speaker who "wows" her audience, Jan Janzen is a dynamic speaker with passion, energy and wisdom to share! Her message is a combination of 'real world' knowledge, coupled with a huge desire to reach people's hearts and motivate them to long-term success.

Networking organizations, corporations, charity events, and churches are welcome to call. Opportunities to create revenue-producing events for your organization are available.

For more information on Jan as a speaker, please visit
www.janjanzen.com

To have Jan Janzen appear live at your next event, please email
speaker@janjanzen.com
or call **1-866-552-6536**

Want to make a difference in the world WHILE running a successful and ethical business?

Shel Horowitz, Founder, is looking for 25,000 entrepreneurs to take the Ethical Business Pledge so together, we can change history!

Check out the Business Ethics Pledge at
www.business-ethics-pledge.org

For more information on microfinancing, and how this book is supporting entrepreneurs in developing countries, please go to www.spiritualentrepreneurinfo.com to learn more about this powerful tool to eradicate poverty.